SNAP HAPPY

BYRON FLITSCH

Printed in the United States of America
First Printing, 2023
ISBN 979-8-218-21592-7
You Are Here Mindfulness Publications
Altadena, CA

SnapHappyMindfulPhotography.com

Flitsch, Byron, author.
Snap Happy: Mindful Photography for Kids/by Byron Flitsch
ISBN 979-8-218-21592-7 (softcover)
1. Photography 2. Hobbies
LCCN 2023907987 (print)

THIS BOOK IS DEDICATED TO...

MY ALWAYS SUPPORTIVE
PARENTS FOR GETTING MY
FIRST CAMERA.
MY SPARKY FOR LETTING ME
TAKE
SNAPS WHEREVER I GO
AND TO CURIOUS SHUTTERBUGS
EVERYWHERE.

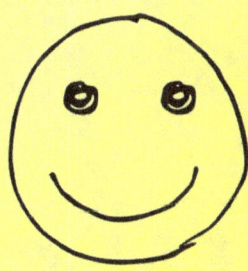

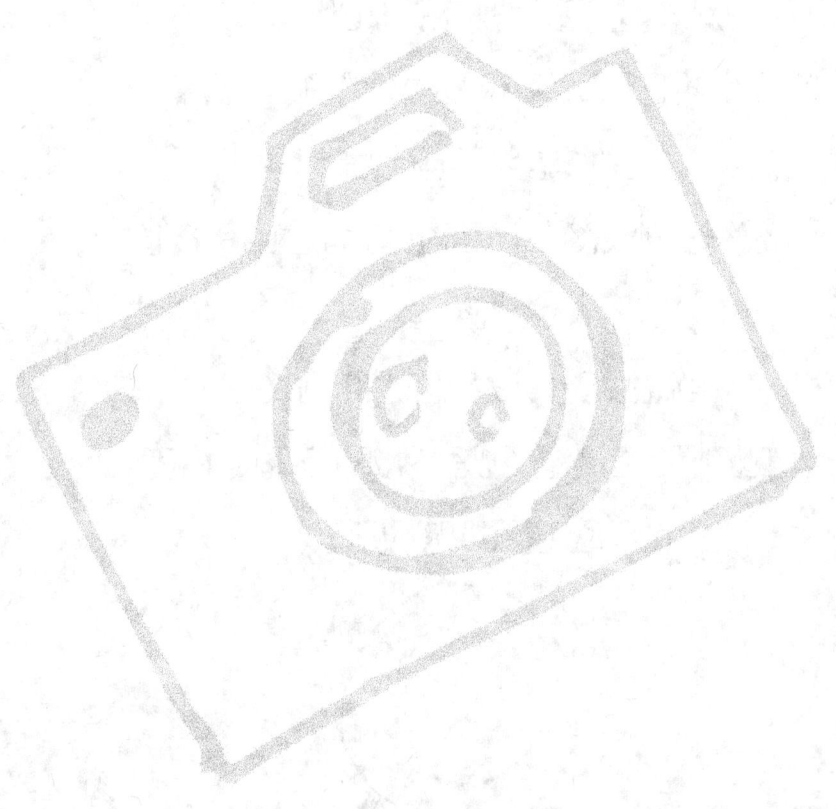

TABLE OF CONTENTS

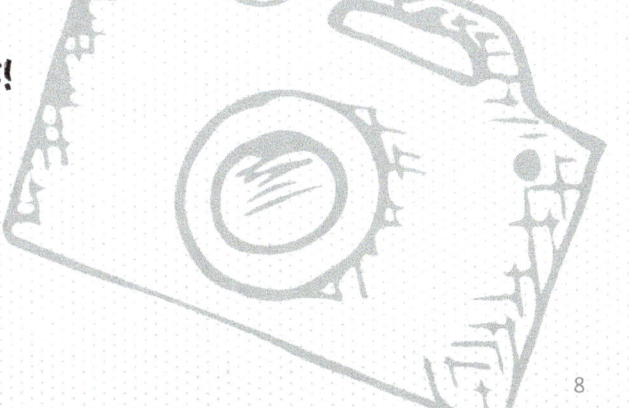

INTENTION

WHAT IS YOUR ==INTENTION?==

BEFORE STARTING ANY NEW PRACTICE, SETTING AN INTENTION WILL GUIDE YOU THROUGH YOUR ADVENTURE. WHAT DO YOU WANT OUT OF THIS BOOK AND EXPERIENCE?

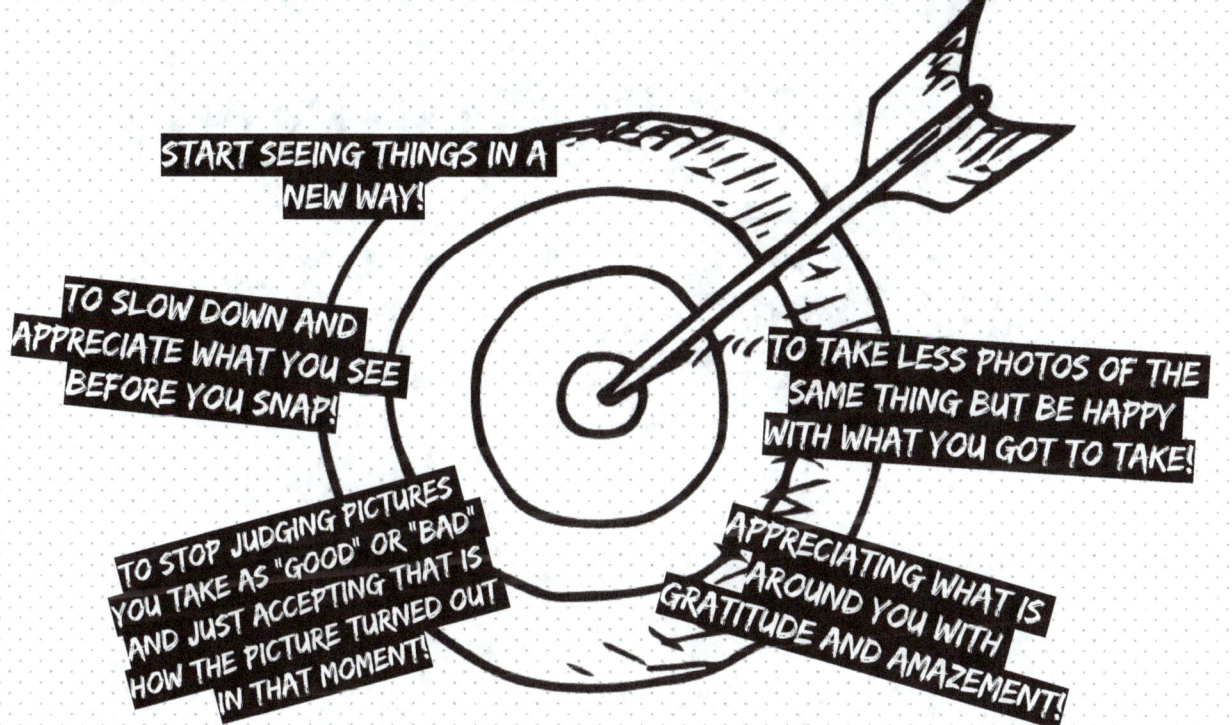

START SEEING THINGS IN A NEW WAY!

TO SLOW DOWN AND APPRECIATE WHAT YOU SEE BEFORE YOU SNAP!

TO TAKE LESS PHOTOS OF THE SAME THING BUT BE HAPPY WITH WHAT YOU GOT TO TAKE!

TO STOP JUDGING PICTURES YOU TAKE AS "GOOD" OR "BAD" AND JUST ACCEPTING THAT IS HOW THE PICTURE TURNED OUT IN THAT MOMENT!

APPRECIATING WHAT IS AROUND YOU WITH GRATITUDE AND AMAZEMENT!

(PSST, YOUR GOALS COULD BE DIFFERENT FROM THESE, TOO!)

What's your Intention?
What do you hope to get out of this experience?
Write it here:

LET'S GET STARTED!

HOW TO USE THIS BOOK

"We live in a snap happy society, but not everyone snaps happily." Byron Flitsch

TAKING PICTURES IS FUN! I GET IT! BUT THE ART OF TAKING PICTURES CAN SOMETIMES GET AN ITTY-BITTY OBSESSIVE BECAUSE OF HOW EASY IT IS TO USE OUR PHONES TO DOCUMENT EVERYTHING.
SO SOME PEOPLE HAVE BECOME SNAP HAPPY, TAKING PICTURES OF EVERYTHING AND ANYTHING WITHOUT REALLY CONNECTING WITH THOSE PHOTOS. BUT, IN THE END, THEY AREN'T REALLY HAPPY WITH THE PROCESS OF TAKING PICTURES OR EVEN HOW THE PICTURES LOOK. ENTER, THIS BOOK!

TIP 1:

LISTEN, WE DON'T MAKE THE RULES AROUND HERE. WAIT, WE KINDA DO. BUT HERE'S THE DEAL: YOU CAN FOLLOW THIS BOOK FROM COVER TO COVER AND JUMP AROUND. YOU CAN DO ONE MISSION A DAY OR SPEND AN ENTIRE MONTH DEVOTED TO ONE MISSION. THE WORLD IS YOUR OYSTER, YO!

TIP 2:

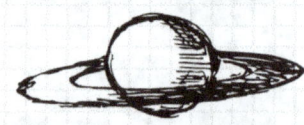

TRY EVERY SINGLE MISSION AT 100%, AND TRY TO BE NICE TO YOURSELF. SOME OF THE ADVENTURES ARE GOING TO BE EASIER THAN OTHERS. SOME OF THEM ARE GONNA MAKE YOU SAY, "HUH?" AND SOME OF THEM ARE GOING TO DRIVE YOU NUTS. AND SOME OF THEM WILL MAKE YOU BREAKDANCE DOWN THE STREET IN EXCITEMENT. BUT TRY ALL OF THEM AT YOUR BEST. GIVE THEM A CHANCE. AND, OF COURSE, MAKE THEM YOUR OWN.

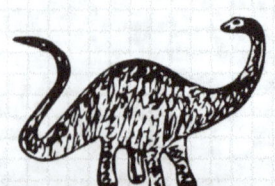

WHAT KIND OF CAMERA YOU USE ==DOESN'T MATTER!==

FIRST, IT'S IMPORTANT TO BE GRATEFUL THAT YOU HAVE A CAMERA AT ALL!

NEXT, HAVING THE BEST CAMERA EVER CREATED MAY ALLOW PHOTOGRAPHERS TO TAKE CERTAIN KINDS OF PICTURES, BUT THAT'S NOT IMPORTANT RIGHT NOW. IF YOUR CAMERA CAN CREATE AN IMAGE, IT IS AMAZING FOR MINDFUL PHOTOGRAPHY!

What cameras are there?

Polaroid/Instant

Cell phone

DSLR

Tablet

Try using old film 35mm cameras or disposable cameras!

NOW, LET'S GET WEIRD: GO GRAB YOUR CAMERA. YES! RIGHT NOW! HOLD YOUR CAMERA IN YOUR HAND AND REPEAT AFTER ME:

"HI, CAMERA. IT'S ME (SAY YOUR NAME). THANK YOU FOR WORKING WITH ME AS I EXPLORE THE WORLD. I AM GRATEFUL FOR YOU."

NOW PET YOUR CAMERA AND GO TAKE YOUR CAMERA OUT FOR A WALK. JUST KIDDING. THAT WOULD BE WEIRD.

THE BASICS

OK, LET'S JUST SAY THIS: THIS ISN'T GONNA BE YOUR INTRO TO TRADITIONAL PHOTOGRAPHY KINDA PLACE. WHILE LEARNING THE TECHNICAL PARTS OF PHOTOGRAPHY CAN BE FUN AND VALUABLE TO CREATING ART, YOU'RE GOING TO HAVE TO FIND THAT SOMEWHERE ELSE. THIS BOOK IS GOING TO FOCUS ON MINDFUL PROCESS AND THE BEAUTY THAT COMES FROM THAT.

SO, THERE ARE SOME BASICS OF PHOTOGRAPHY THAT EVERYONE SHOULD KNOW (SO WE CAN BREAK THEM LATER!) UGH, RULES! BUT RULES ARE MADE TO BE BROKEN — SHH, I DIDN'T TELL YOU THAT.

RULE OF THIRDS

BASICALLY, YOUR EYES ARE TRAINED IN A CERTAIN WAY TO LOOK AT IMAGES WHERE THE SUBJECT MATCHES UP TO THESE IMAGINARY LINES THAT INTERSECT IN COMPOSITIONS. SCIENCE!

TEXTURE

CATCHING A SUBJECT JUST AT THE RIGHT ANGLE CAN ALLOW US TO ALMOST FEEL WHAT IT WOULD FEEL LIKE TO TOUCH IT.

FOCUS

JUST LIKE OUR EYES, THE LENS OF A CAMERA LIKES TO SEE EVERYTHING AND TENDS TO GET A LITTLE BLURRY WHEN IT'S NOT ENTIRELY CONCENTRATING ON ONE THING. FOCUS ALLOWS US TO SHARPEN IN ON OUR SUBJECT.

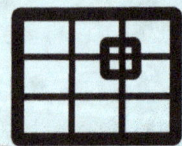

PATTERN

REPETITIVE SHAPES OR LINES CREATE A PATTERN. THEY ARE EVERYWHERE!

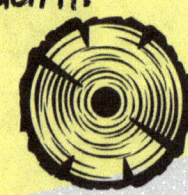

15

PARTS OF THE BOOK!

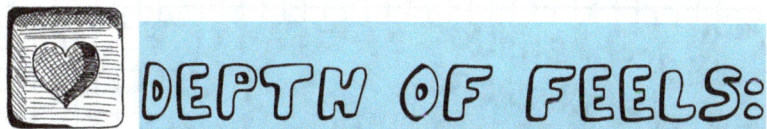 **FOCUS:** THESE ARE GOING TO BE YOUR ASSIGNMENTS OR WHAT MINDFUL PHOTOGRAPHY SKILL YOU WILL FOCUS ON.

DEPTH OF FEELS: IN PHOTOGRAPHY, IT'S CALLED "DEPTH OF FIELD," MEANING THE DISTANCE BETWEEN THE NEAREST AND THE FURTHEST OBJECTS.

BUT DEPTH OF FEELS IS MORE A REFLECTION OF THE ACTIVITY. PART OF BEING MINDFUL AND AN ARTIST IS TO THINK ABOUT YOUR PROCESS. THIS WILL BE LIKE A LITTLE JOURNAL MOMENT.

Taking pictures of

clouds made me feel

relaxed because they

were always changing

just like how I am.

DOCUMENT YOUR STUDIES!

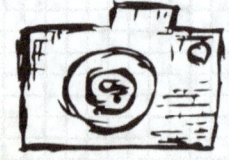

PORTFOLIO

PLACES TO GLUE OR TAPE IN YOUR PRINTED PHOTOGRAPHS TO DOCUMENT YOUR EXPERIENCE!

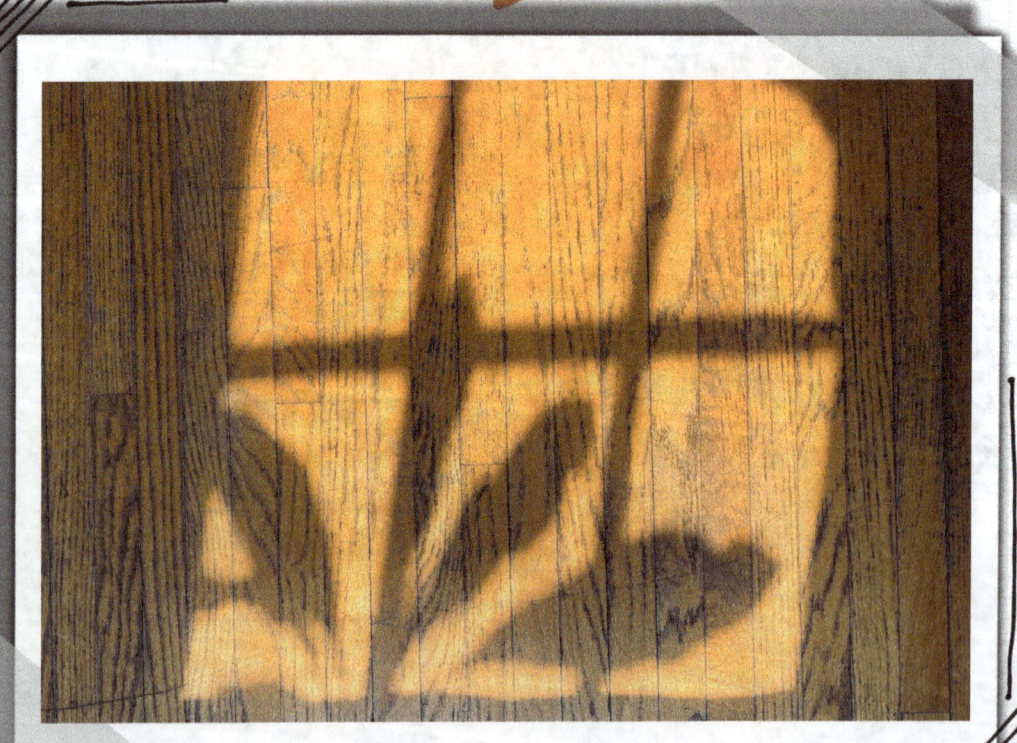

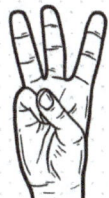

PARTS OF MINDFULNESS

Your Focus Assignments are broken up in to three styles: <mark>Attention, Intention & Attitude</mark>

ATTENTION

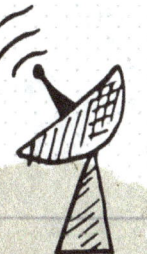

PAY ATTENTION TO WHAT YOU ARE FEELING INSIDE OR OUTSIDE OF YOUR BODY. YOU PRACTICE THIS BY REFLECTING, WHICH IS JUST A FANCY WAY OF THINKING ABOUT WHAT YOU DO, HOW YOU DO IT, AND WHY. WHAT DOES YOUR BODY FEEL WHEN YOU DO SOMETHING, PHYSICALLY, EMOTIONALLY, AND MENTALLY?

INTENTION

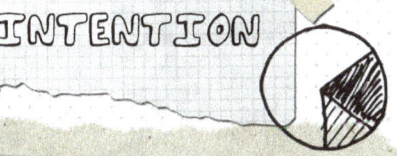

INTENTION IS WHAT YOU WANT TO GET OUT OF YOUR PRACTICE. DO YOU WANT TO SEE THE BEAUTY OF THE WORLD MORE? DO YOU WANT TO BE CREATIVE WITHOUT FEELING LIKE PEOPLE AREN'T GOING TO LIKE WHAT YOU MAKE? DO YOU JUST WANT TO EXPLORE? DO YOU WANT TO FEEL MORE THANKFUL FOR BEING ABLE TO MAKE AWESOME THINGS? WHAT IS YOUR GOAL?

ATTITUDE

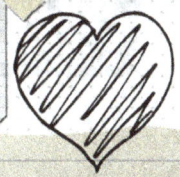

ATTITUDE IN MINDFULNESS MEANS BEING SASSY. JUST KIDDING! IT MEANS ASKING YOURSELF HOW YOU WANT TO SEE THINGS. THERE ARE ACTUALLY SEVEN ATTITUDES THAT A COOL GUY NAMED JON KABAT-ZINN (FULL CATASTROPHE LIVING) 1990 SAYS EXIST: PATIENCE, KINDNESS, CURIOSITY, ACCEPTANCE, FREEDOM TO LET GO OF CONTROL, NOT BEING A JUDGY-WUDGY BEAR, AND TO COOL IT WITH THE EXPECTATIONS.

RIGHT & LEFT BRAIN

A LITTLE NEUROSCIENCE FOR YA! (THAT'S THE STUDY OF THE BRAIN, BTW). IT IS BELIEVED THAT WE HAVE TWO SIDES OF OUR BRAIN AND THAT WE ACCESS THOSE PARTS FOR DIFFERENT SKILLS.

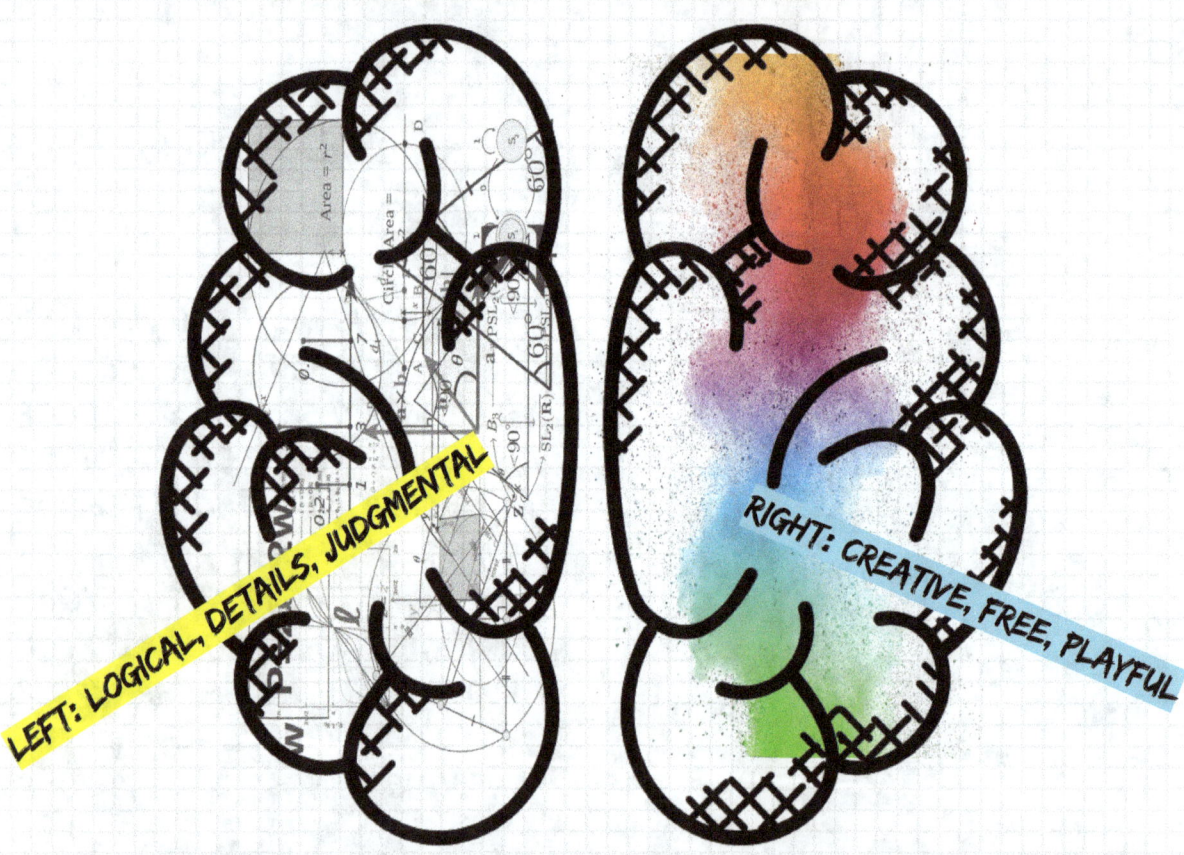

LEFT: LOGICAL, DETAILS, JUDGMENTAL

RIGHT: CREATIVE, FREE, PLAYFUL

BECAUSE A LOT OF TECH AND THINKING GOES INTO TAKING A PICTURE, MANY PHOTOGRAPHERS ARE OFTEN LIVING IN THE LEFT SIDE OF THE BRAIN: ANALYTICAL, LOGICAL, STEP-BY-STEP. BUT AS AN ARTIST, THERE IS DABBING INTO THE RIGHT TO COMPOSE AND EXPRESS MOTION.

BUT FOR THIS BOOK, WE ARE FOCUSING MORE ON THE RIGHT. WE ARE USING THE CAMERA AS A TOOL TO EXPRESS OURSELVES WITHOUT JUDGMENT FOR WHAT IS GOOD OR BAD IN PHOTOGRAPHY AND NOT SO MUCH FOCUSING ON THE TECHNICAL.

THIS BOOK IS ABOUT BREAKING THE RULES (SHHHHH, ACTUALLY, NO! DON'T KEEP THAT QUIET! LET'S BREAK SOME RULES! AND LEARNING ABOUT OURSELVES ALONG THE WAY!

OH SNAP! PHOTO FOR THOUGHT!

GUESS WHAT? YOU'RE NOT GONNA BE THE BEST PHOTOGRAPHER RIGHT AWAY. JUST LIKE LEARNING PIANO, THROWING A FOOTBALL, OR LEARNING HOW TO SPEAK PIG LATIN. IT TAKES TIME AND EXPLORATION!

BUT YOU MAY GET FRUSTRATED FROM THIS BOOK BECAUSE SOMETIMES PEOPLE FEEL LIKE THEIR PICTURE, EXPERIENCE, MOOD, TIMING, COLOR, ALL OF IT COULD HAVE BEEN BETTER ONLY

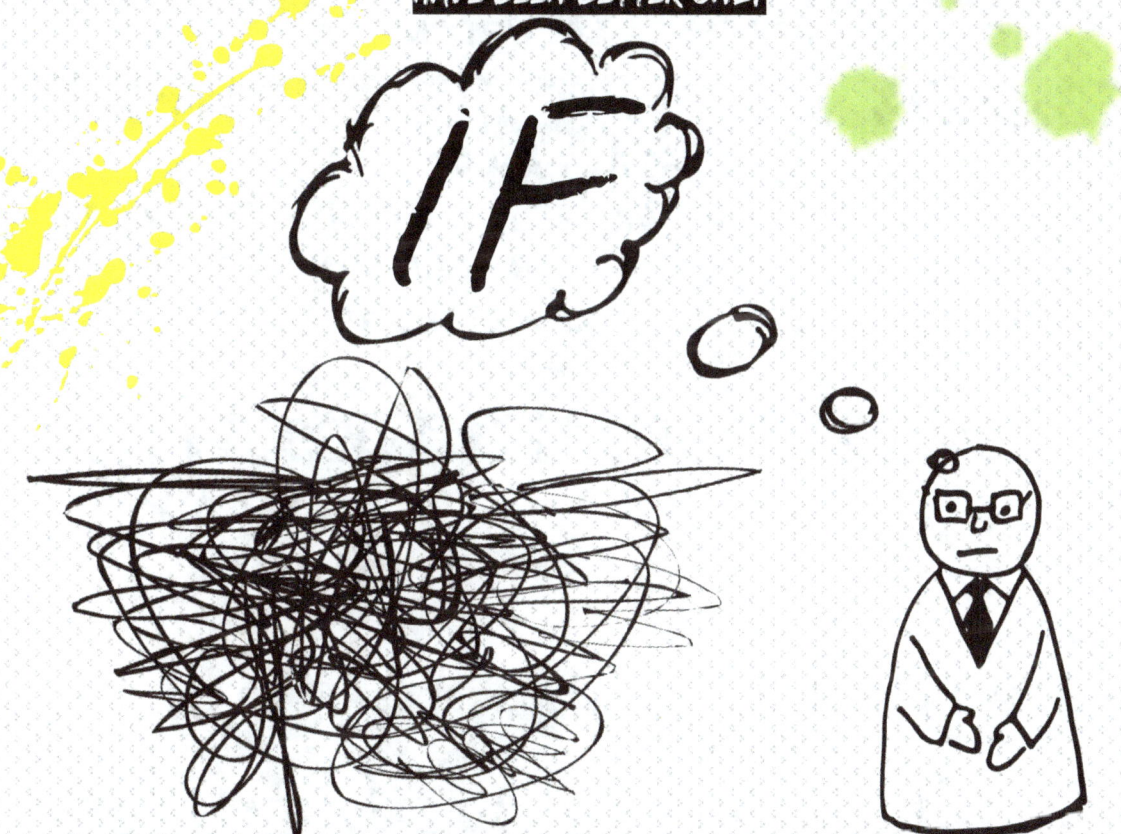

THAT WORD "IF" IS A BIGGIE. IT ASKS US TO THINK OF EVERY OTHER THING WE COULD DO TO TAKE A BETTER PICTURE INSTEAD OF WHAT WE DID DO! THAT WORD GIVES US ANXIETY AND THAT'S NOT FUN!

NOW, SHOULD WE ALWAYS BE LEARNING AND EVOLVING OUR STYLE? SURE. BUT WHEN YOU TAKE A PICTURE, AND IT DOESN'T TURN OUT HOW YOU PLANNED, INSTEAD OF ASKING "IF," REMIND YOURSELF OF THE POSITIVES AND SET A GOAL OF ONE THING YOU WILL TRY NEXT TIME.

APPRECIATE THE JOURNEY, NOT THE DESTINATION!

SHELFIE THE SELFIE

OK, HERE'S THE DEAL, FRIEND: SELFIES ARE OK ONCE IN A WHILE. THEY CAN BE FUN, YOU CAN BE SILLY, AND YOU GET TO PRACTICE SEEING HOW OTHERS SEE YOUR FACE. BUT: THERE HAVE BEEN STUDIES DONE ABOUT SELFIES, AND IT LOOKS LIKE THEY MAY BE CAUSING US SOME ANXIETY ABOUT OUR APPEARANCE AND PLAYING WITH OUR CONFIDENCE A BIT. WE DON'T WANT THAT!

SO, LET'S SEE IF WE CAN SHELF THE SELFIE FOR A WHOLE MONTH. A WHOLE MONTH?!

I SWEAR I'M NOT TRYING TO TORTURE YOU. BUT I DO WANT YOU TO START SEEING THE CAMERA AS AN EXTENSION OF YOUR EYE — SORT OF LIKE A COOL TELESCOPE TO EXPLORE THE WORLD AND NOT SO MUCH A MIRROR.

READY TO TAKE THE "SHELF THE SELFIE" PLEDGE?

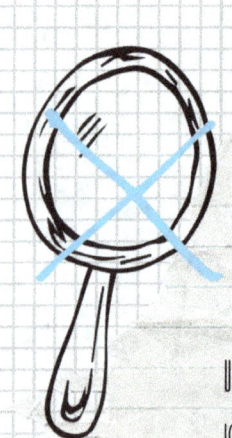

Put your right hand up and repeat these words:

I (Your name) will Shelf the Selfie for one whole month. Even if it gets *realllllly* hard, I'm going to shelf it! Even if my friends try to talk me into it, I'm going to shelf it! The camera is to explore and not to adore!

LET'S GET STARTED!

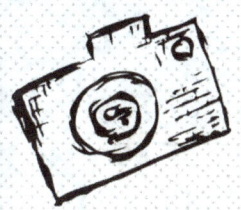

LET'S REVIEW!

T OR F   MINDFUL PHOTOGRAPHY SHOULD BE REALLY STRESSFUL.

T OR F   THE TYPE OF CAMERA MATTERS WHEN EXPLORING MINDFUL PHOTOGRAPHY.

T OR F   I SHOULD GIVE MY CAMERA A NAME!

T OR F   THE RIGHT SIDE OF THE BRAIN IS MORE CREATIVE.

T OR F   I SHOULD TAKE ALL THE SELFIES ALL THE TIME!

T OR F   INTENTION IS TO KNOW WHAT YOU WANT TO GET OUT OF YOUR PRACTICE.

T OR F   YOU SHOULD USE THIS BOOK HOWEVER WAY YOU'D LIKE!

T OR F   THE WORD "PORTFOLIO" COMES FROM ITALY (SAY: PORTAFOGLIO).

T OR F   RULES OF THIRD IS NOT PART OF TAKING PICTURES.

T OR F   I AM EXCITED TO START SNAPPING HAPPILY!

Answers: F, F, T, T, F, T, T, T, F, T

TIME TO GET OUR SNAP ON!

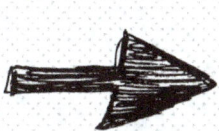
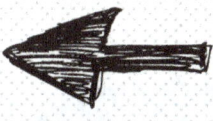

THINK ABOUT IT!

AS YOUR START YOUR ADVENTURE, WHAT ARE YOU MOST EXCITED ABOUT? WHAT ARE YOU CURIOUS ABOUT? WHAT DO YOU HOPE TO LEARN FROM THIS BOOK?

"THE CAMERA GAVE ME AN INCREDIBLE FREEDOM. IT GAVE ME THE ABILITY TO PARADE THROUGH THE WORLD AND LOOK AT PEOPLE AND THINGS VERY CLOSELY."

— CARRIE MAE WEEMS

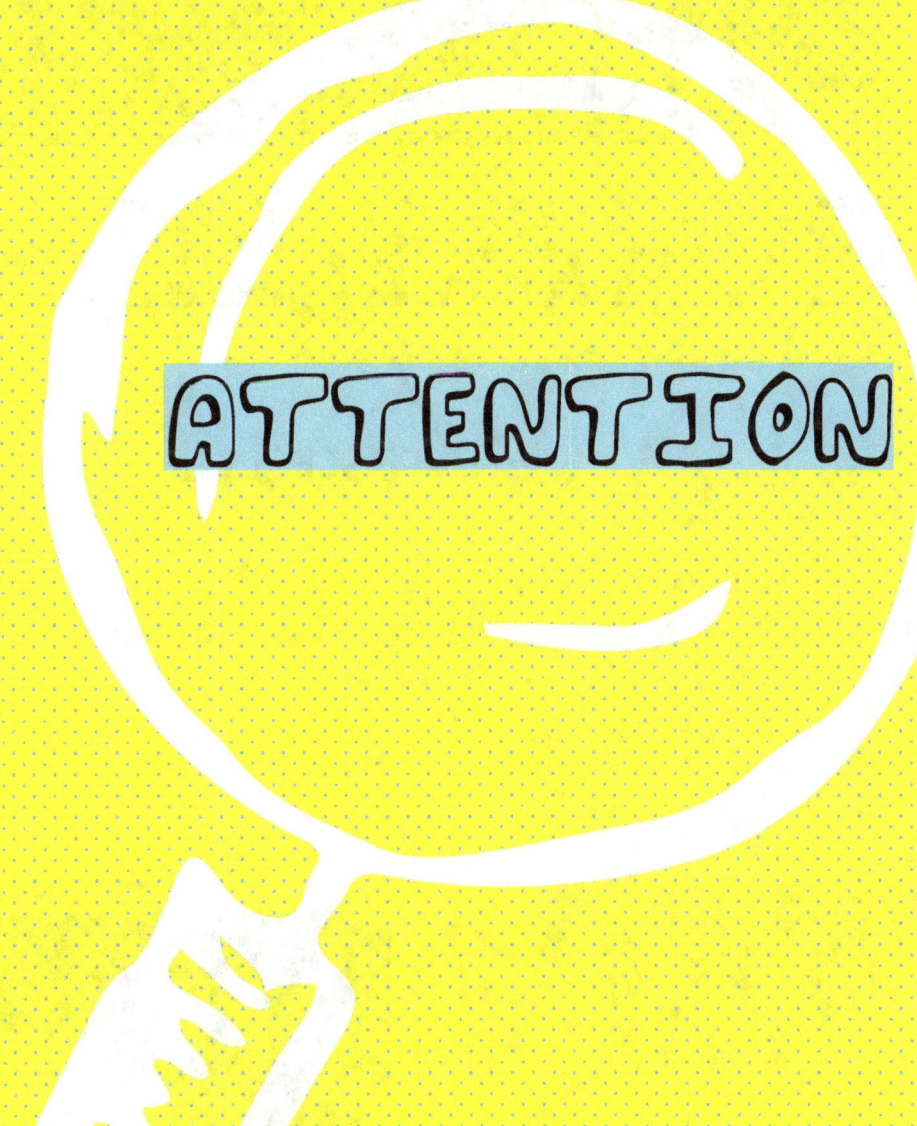

ATTENTION

FOCUS : BE A SHAPE SEEKER

SHAPES ARE EVERYWHERE, AND SOMETIMES WE DON'T EVEN REALIZE IT! THEY MAKE UP PRETTY MUCH EVERY PART OF OUR WORLD. LET'S SLOW DOWN AND SEEK THE SHAPES!

EVERY DAY PICK A DIFFERENT SHAPE TO FOCUS ON. BELOW IS A SCHEDULE, BUT YOU DO YOU BOO — PICK ANY SHAPE FOR ANY DAY!

MY SHAPE SCHEDULE

Monday -- Circles ◯
Tuesday -- Squares ☐
Wednesday -- Triangles △
Thursday -- Stars ☆

Friday -- Rectangles ☐
Saturday -- Diamond ◇
Sunday -- Ovals ◯

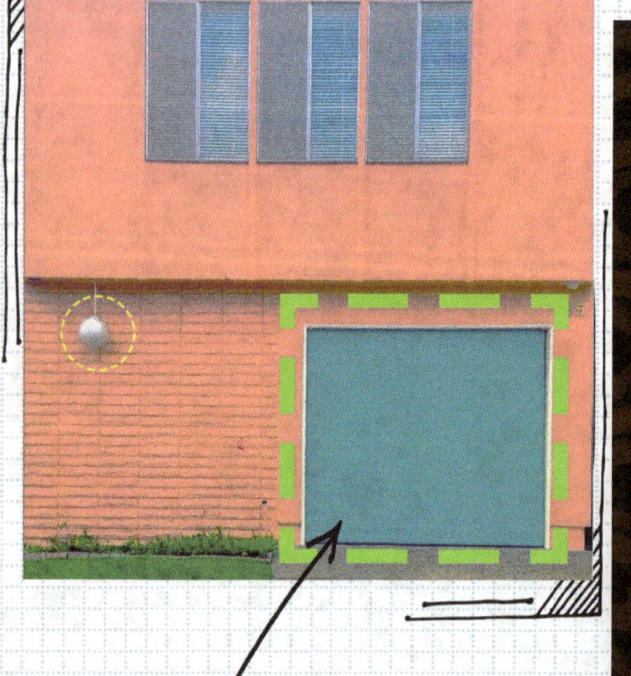

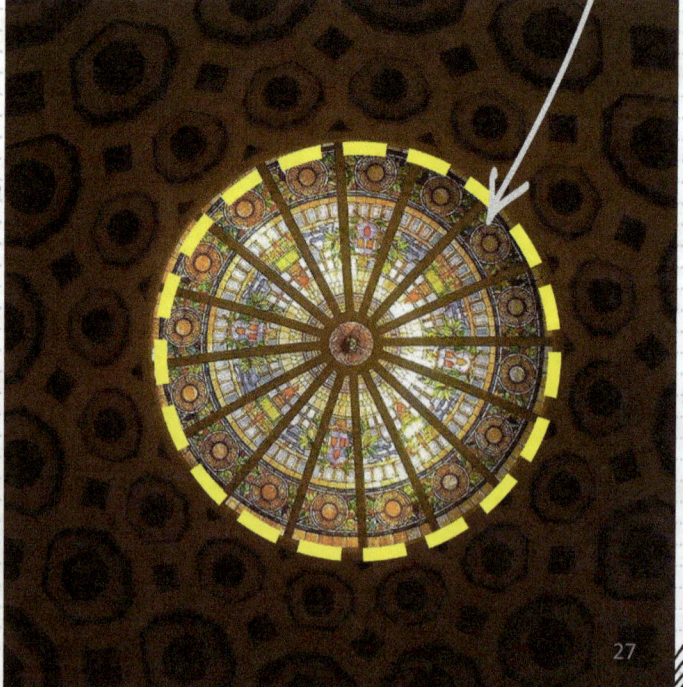

FOCUS : BE A SHAPE SEEKER

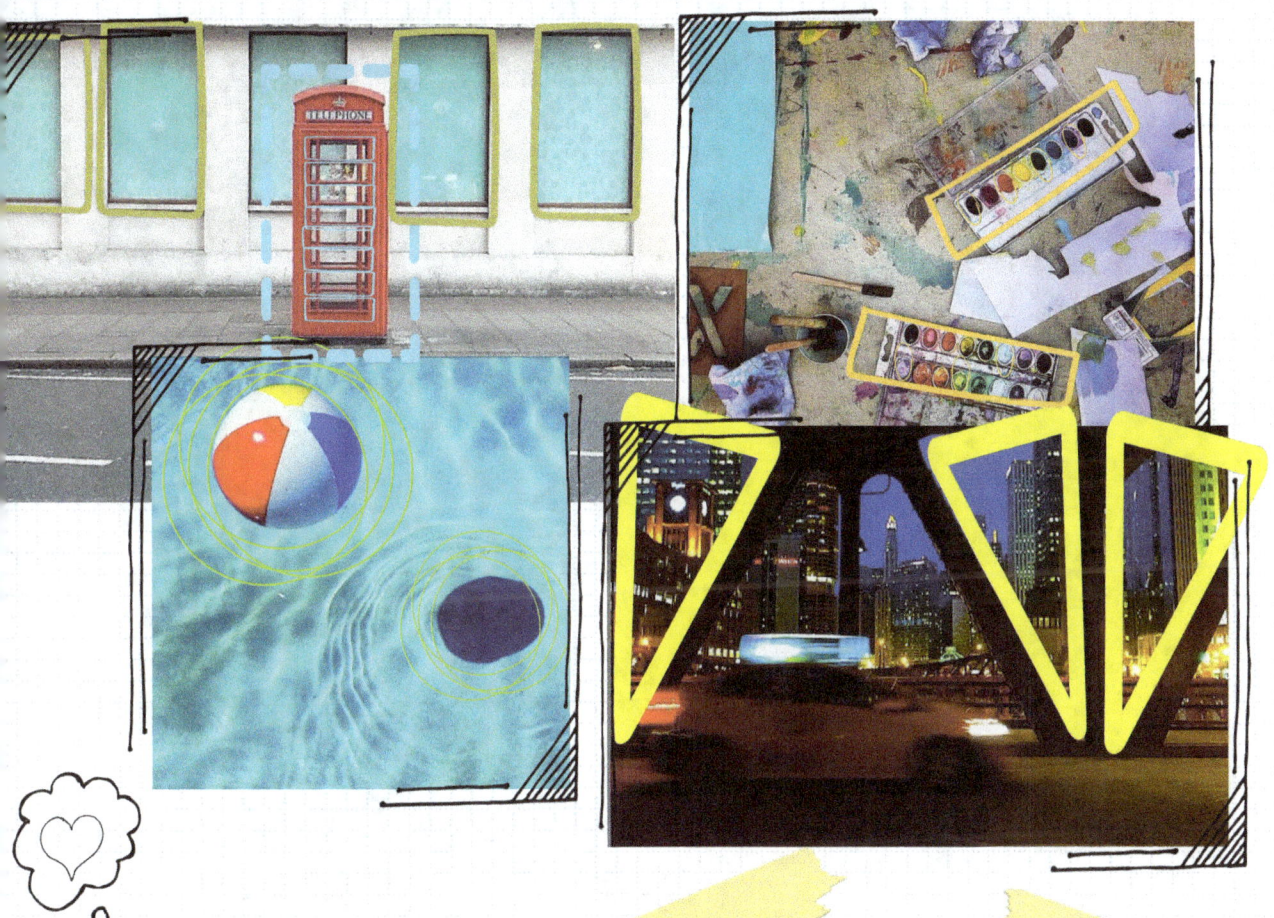

DEPTH OF FEELS:

WAS THIS FUN? CIRCLE

YES OR NO

WHAT DID YOU ENJOY ABOUT SHAPE
HUNTING? WHY?

WHAT WASN'T EASY? WHY?

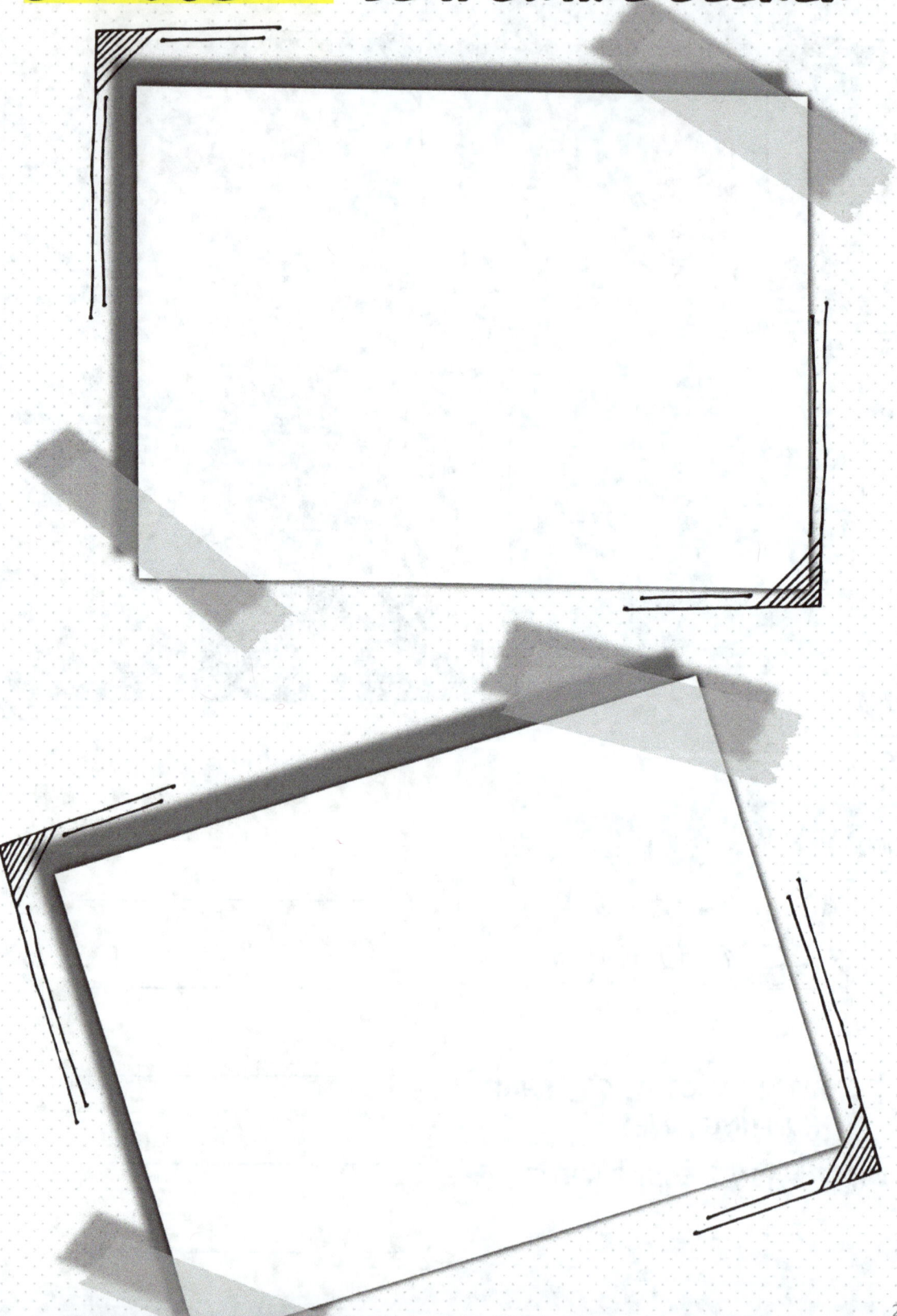

FOCUS : 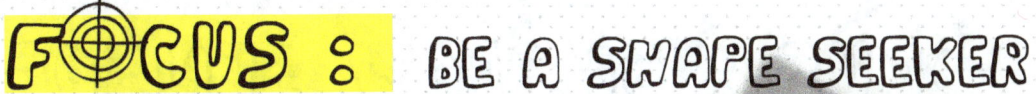 BE A SHAPE SEEKER

F⊕CUS : SHADOW SENSOR

WHAT IF I TOLD YOU A WHOLE OTHER WORLD EXISTS ON THIS PLANET AND EVEN FOLLOWS YOU WHEREVER YOU GO? CREEPED OUT YET?

DON'T BE! WE'RE TALKING ABOUT SHADOWS!

HAVE YOU EVER JUST STOPPED AND ONLY LOOKED AT SHADOWS? LIKE THE SHAPES OF CLOUDS, THEY OFTEN LOOK LIKE SOMETHING COMPLETELY DIFFERENT THAN WHAT IT REALLY IS.

FOR THIS EXPLORATION, BE MINDFULLY AWARE OF ALL THE SHADOWS. STALK SHADOWS! YOU ARE A SHADOW SLEUTH! SCIENCE TELLS US THAT SHADOWS LOOK DIFFERENT AT DIFFERENT TIMES OF THE DAY SO...

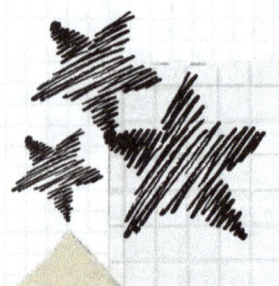

1.) Find one thing around you that has a shadow. Watch that shadow and document it in the morning, afternoon, and later in the day. How does the shadow change? How can you capture its "essence" or personality in a photograph at different times of the day?

2) Take pictures only of shadows all day. Nothing else. Just look for shadows. Create compositions that use shadows to make abstract patterns or document all the shadows you see — every single shadow.

FUN TIP:

TRY PHOTOGRAPHING THESE IN BLACK AND WHITE AND IN COLOR.

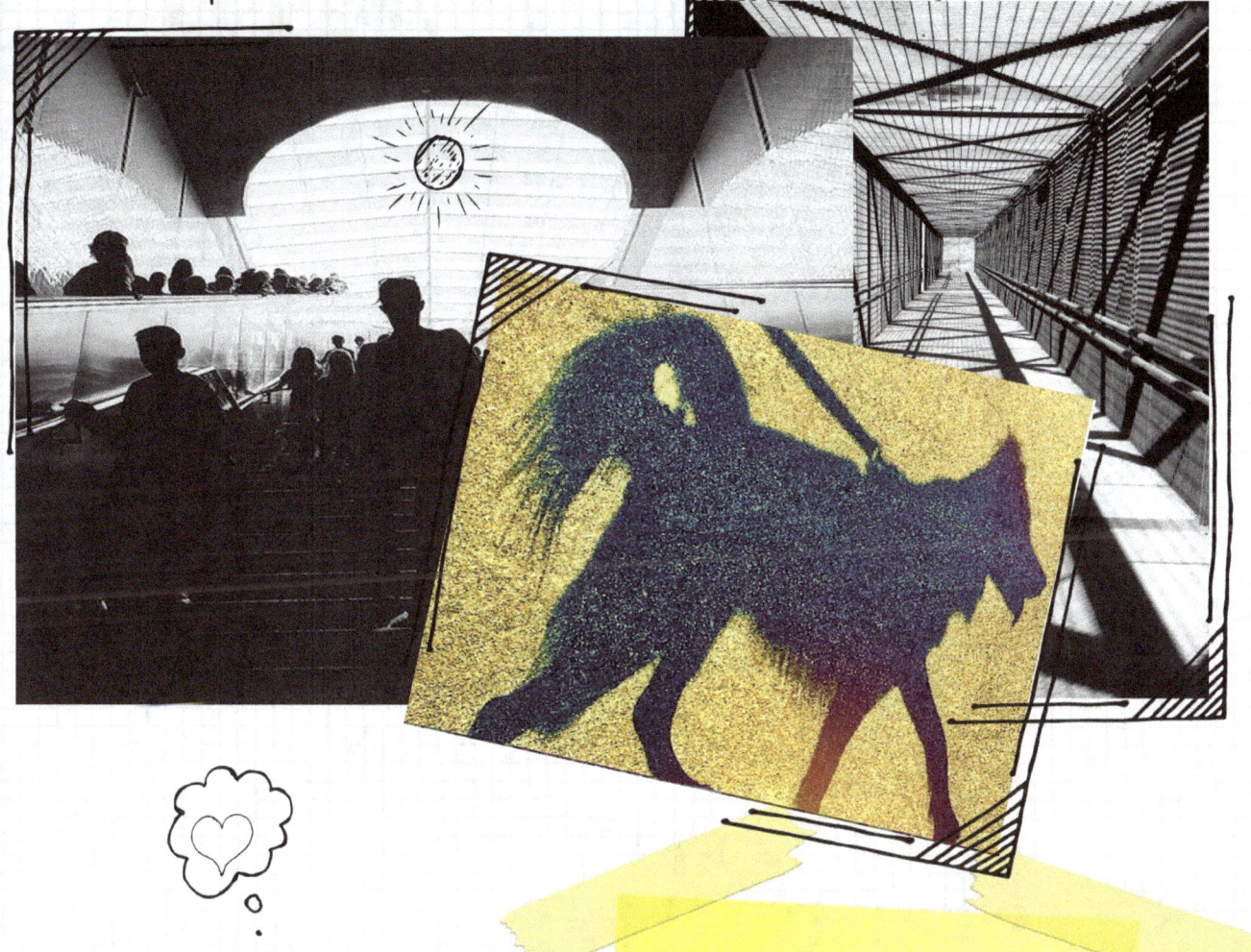

DEPTH OF FEELS:

WAS THIS FUN? CIRCLE

YES OR NO

DID YOU LIKE TAKING SHADOWS IN BLACK AND WHITE, WHY? WHAT FEELING DO YOU GET FROM THAT?

WHAT WAS IT LIKE ONLY LOOKING FOR SHADOWS, SOMETHING WE TEND TO IGNORE EVERY DAY?

FOCUS : SHADOW SENSOR

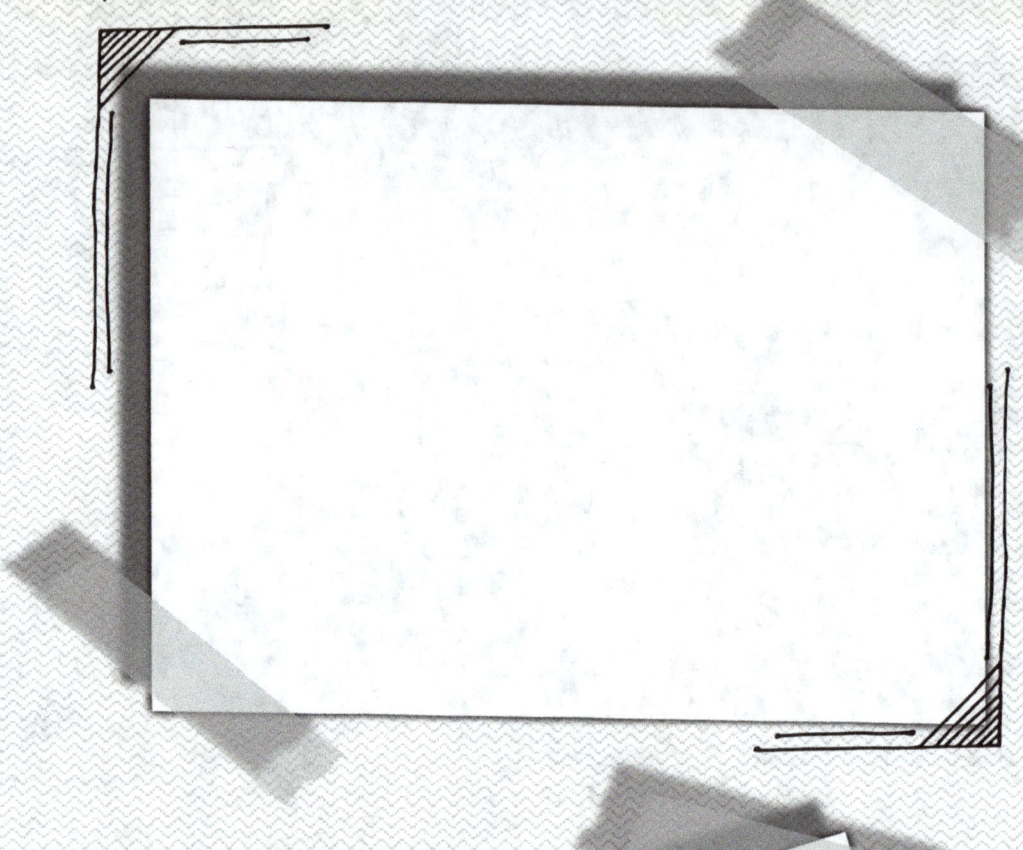

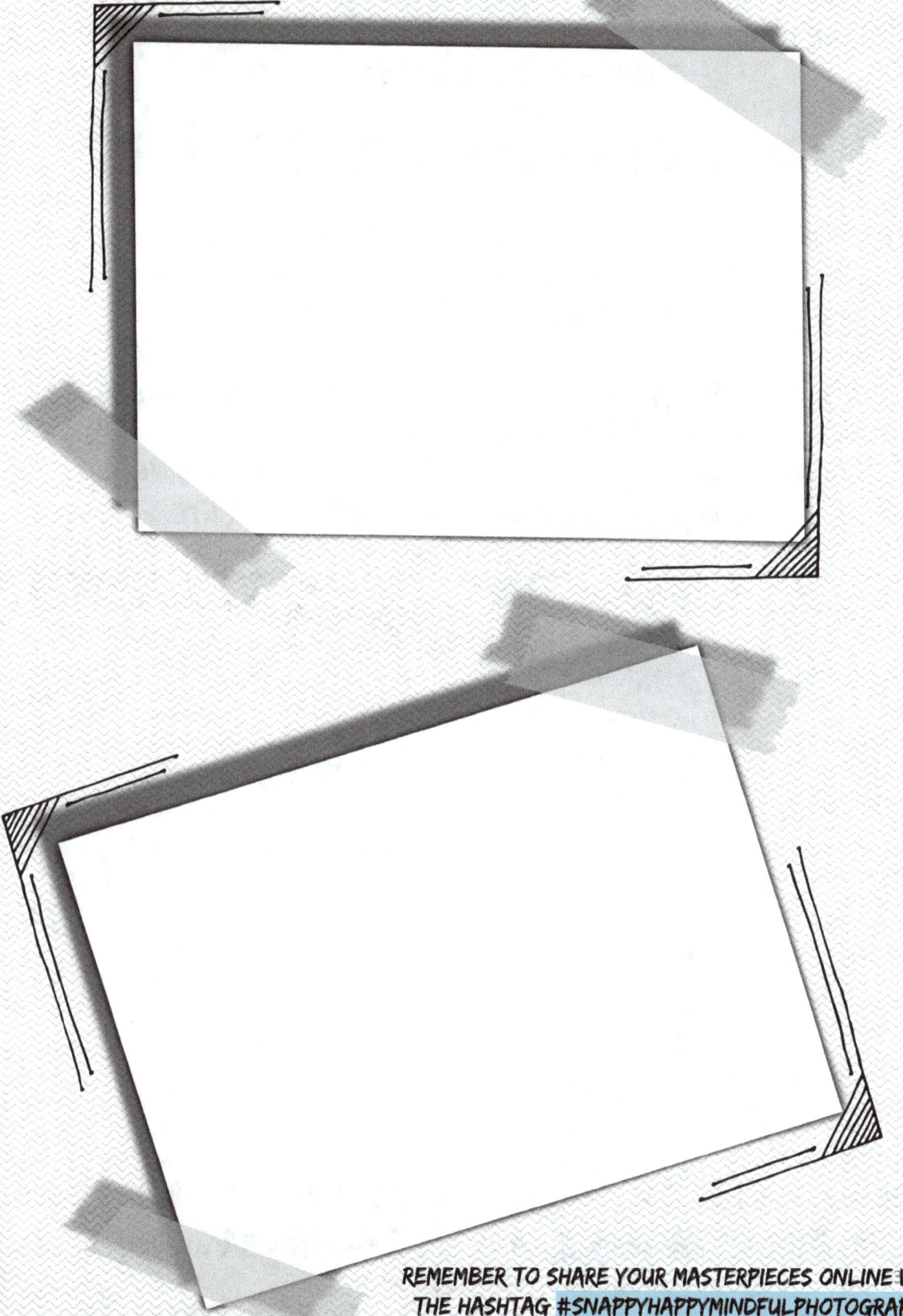

F⊙CUS : SEE THE COLOR!

COLOR IS ALL AROUND US, BUT HAVE YOU EVER SEEN A COLOR SO BEAUTIFUL IF MADE YOU STOP AND STARE?

HOW DOES COLOR IMPACT THE WAY WE SEE THE WORLD?

THE SCIENCE OF COLOR BASICALLY USES LIGHT AND REFLECTION TO CREATE HUES, BUT THOSE HUES CAN ALSO GIVE ALL KINDS OF DIFFERENT FEELS AND EMOTIONS.

DO NOT PHOTOGRAPH NATURE OR WORDS OR SIGNS. LOOK FOR A COLOR THAT EXISTS EVERYWHERE ELSE: ON WALLS, ON THE RIM OF A BICYCLE WHEEL. LOOK FOR BOLD, PUNCHING, SCREAMING, LIKE HUNGRY BABY COLORS THAT CATCH YOUR EYE.

TRY EXPLORING ONE OBJECT (THE SAME OBJECT!) EVERY DAY AT DIFFERENT TIMES OF THE DAY.

Here's your color checklist

- ☐ Red
- ☐ Yellow
- ☐ Blue
- ☐ Purple
- ☐ Orange
- ☐ Black
- ☐ Green
- ☐ White

REMEMBER TO LOOK FOR DIFFERENT VALUES OF COLOR (THAT'S THE FANCY WORD FOR "SHADES" — BRIGHT, DARK, LIGHTER, OR FADED.)

FOCUS : SEE THE COLOR!

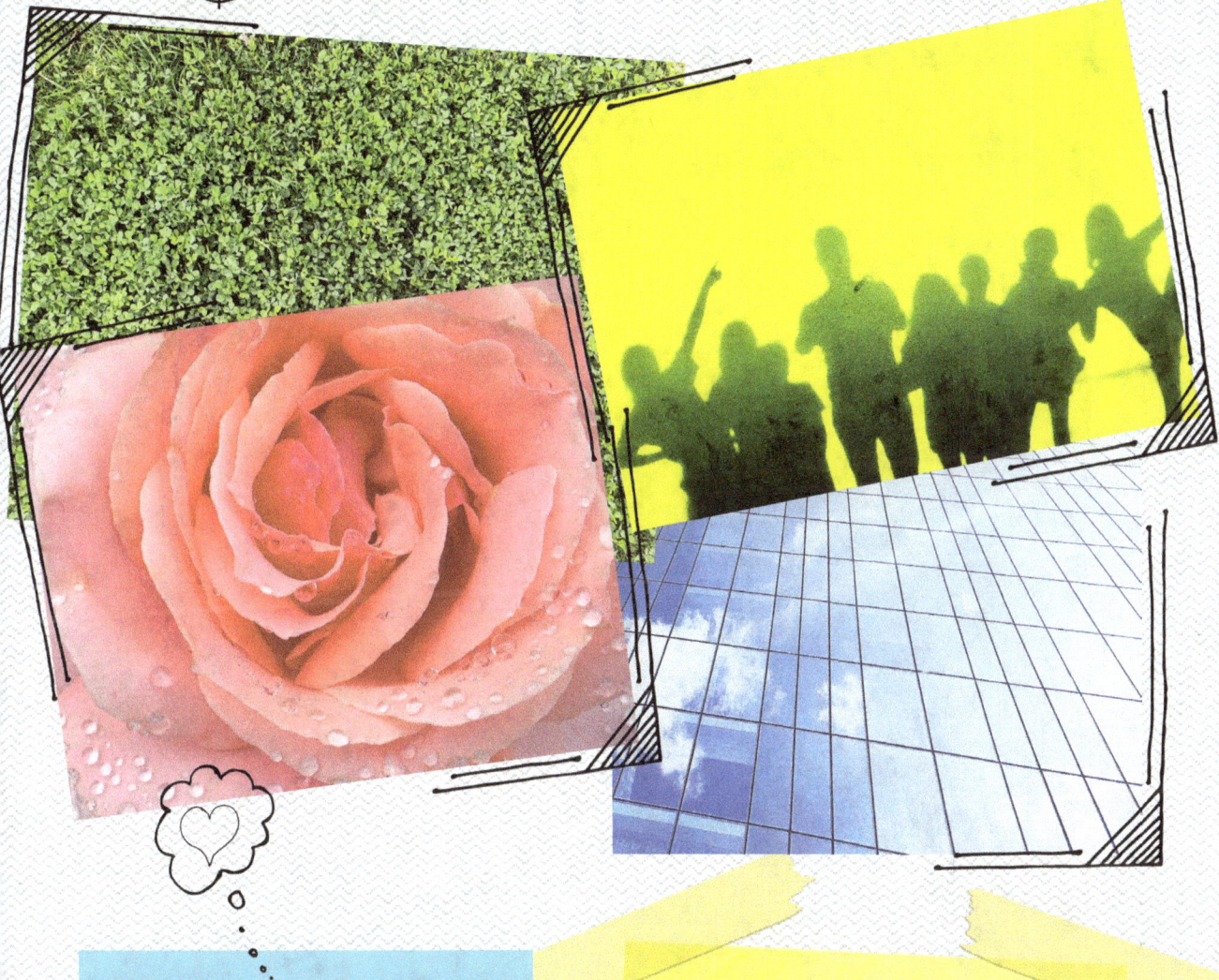

DEPTH OF FEELS:

WAS THIS FUN? CIRCLE

YES OR NO

WHAT COLORS MAKE YOU FEEL
HAPPY? WHICH COLORS MAKE YOU
FEEL SAD?

WHAT WASN'T EASY? WHY?

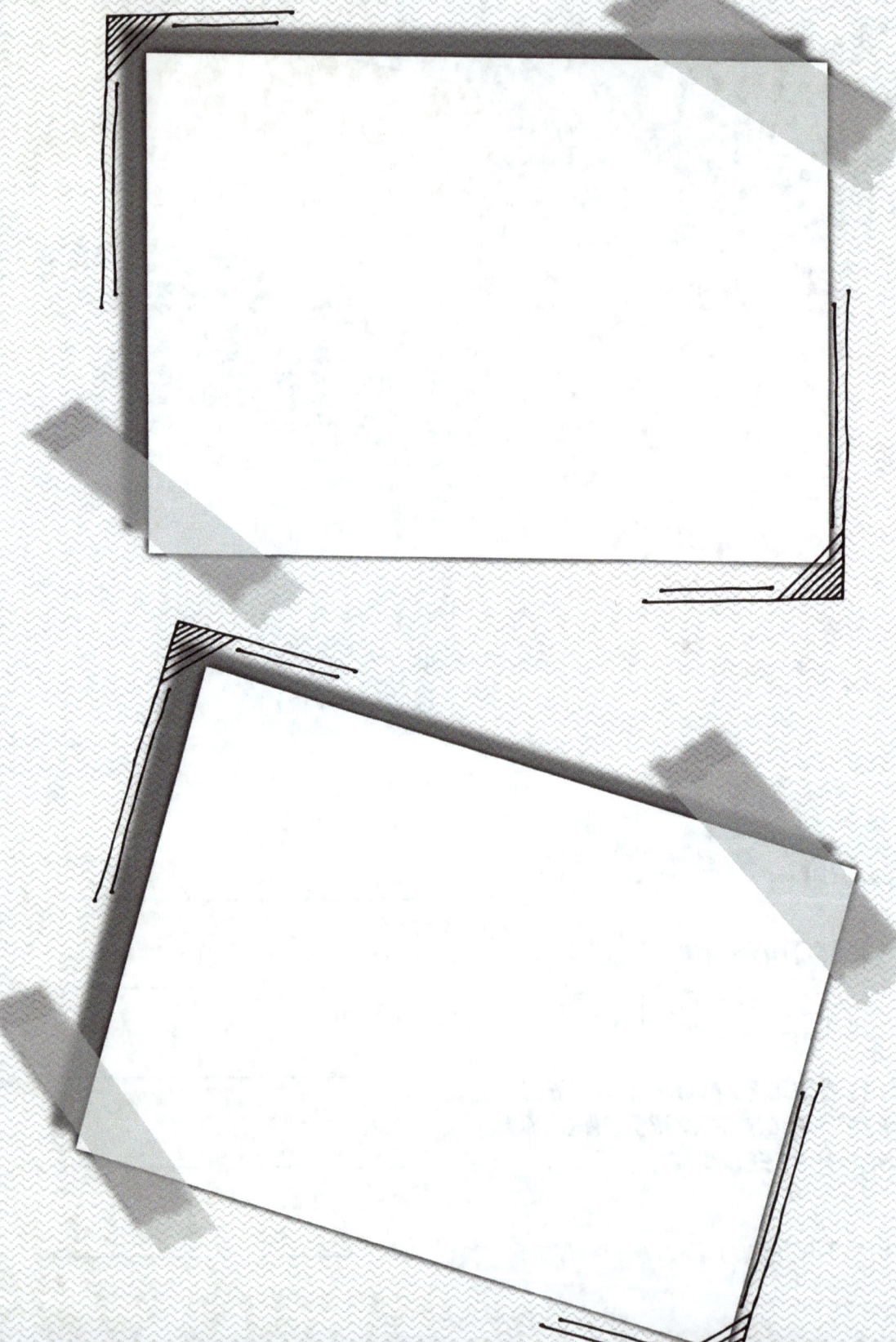

F⊙CUS : SEE THE COLOR!

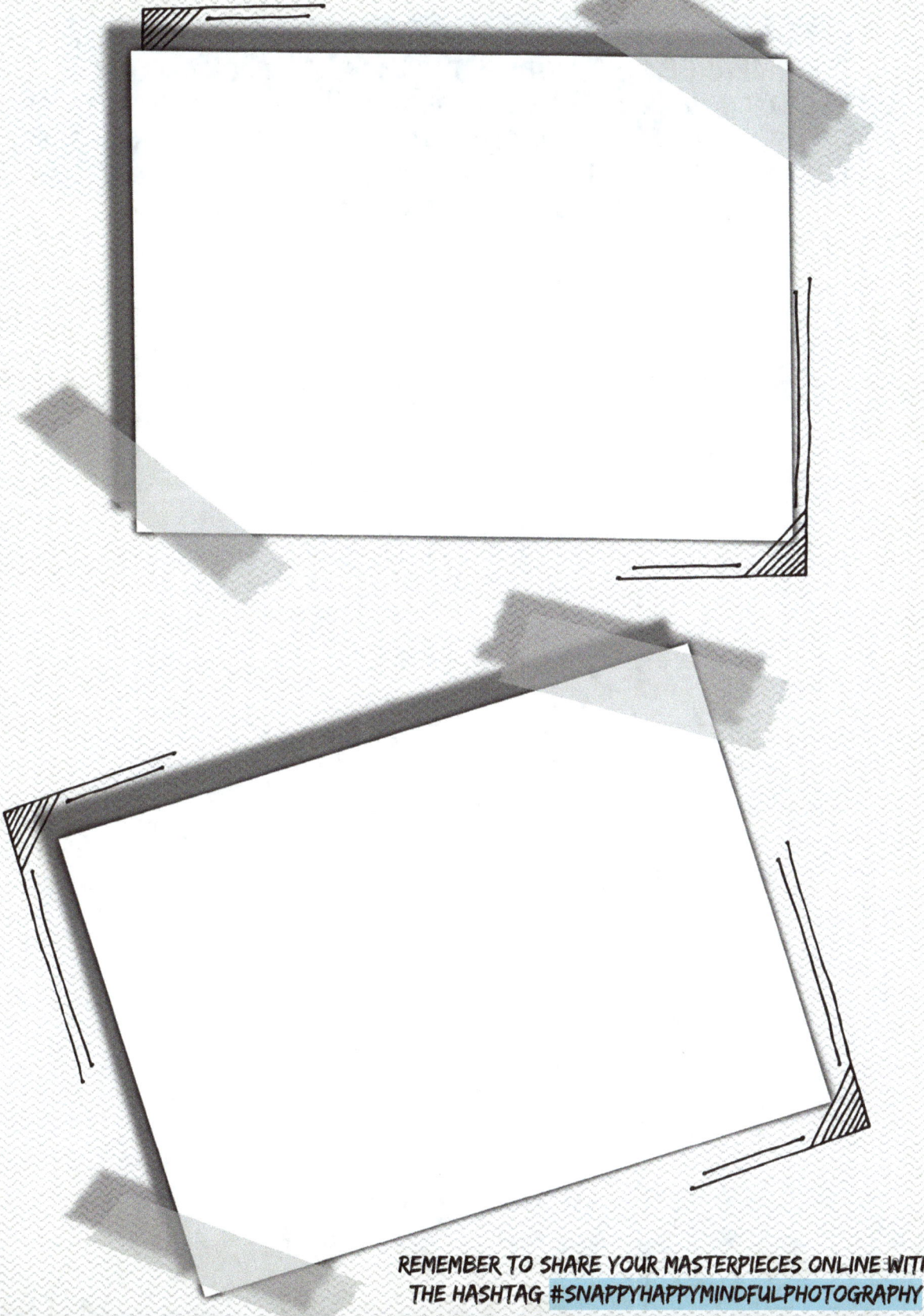

THINK ABOUT IT

USE THIS PAGE TO THINK ABOUT HOW YOU ARE CHANGING BY PRACTICING BEING A MINDFUL PHOTOGRAPHER. DO YOU FEEL DIFFERENT? IF SO, WHAT ARE YOU FEELING? ARE YOU HAVING FUN? WHAT ELSE DO YOU WANT TO GET OUT OF USING THIS BOOK? DRAW, WRITE, OR EVEN CREATE A SECRET CODE BELOW TO REFLECT ON HOW YOU ARE DOING. ARE YOU SNAP HAPPY?

"THE BEST THING ABOUT A PICTURE IS THAT IT NEVER CHANGES, EVEN WHEN THE PEOPLE IN IT DO."

—ANDY WARHOL

FOCUS : REFLECTIONS

WHEN WE PRACTICE SEEING IN A MINDFUL WAY, WE OFTEN START SEEING THINGS WE NEVER NOTICED BEFORE.
WE ALSO NOTICE TEMPORARY THINGS — WE ARE CATCHING THEM HAPPENING, CREATING, OR BEING PRESENT IN THEIR SHORT LIFE SPAN, LIKE REFLECTIONS.

SOMETIMES THE LIGHT HITS THE WINDOW JUST RIGHT, AND YOU SEE A RAINBOW ON A TABLE FROM THE REFLECTION! MAGIC!

SOMETIMES YOU WALK PAST A PUDDLE, AND THE ENTIRE SKY IS REFLECTED AT YOU! MAGIC!

SOMETIMES IT'S A WET STREET, AND A STOP LIGHT'S BRIGHT GREEN IS BOUNCING BACK FROM THE SLIPPERY PAVEMENT. MAGIC!

Your Adventure:

Hunt for reflections:
- In water or puddles
- In mirrors
- In the light

Before snapping them, see what's creating them.

ISN'T IT AWESOME THAT YOU GOT TO WITNESS THIS IMPERMANENT (THAT MEANS NOT PERMANENT!) PIECE OF ART?!

FOCUS : REFLECTIONS

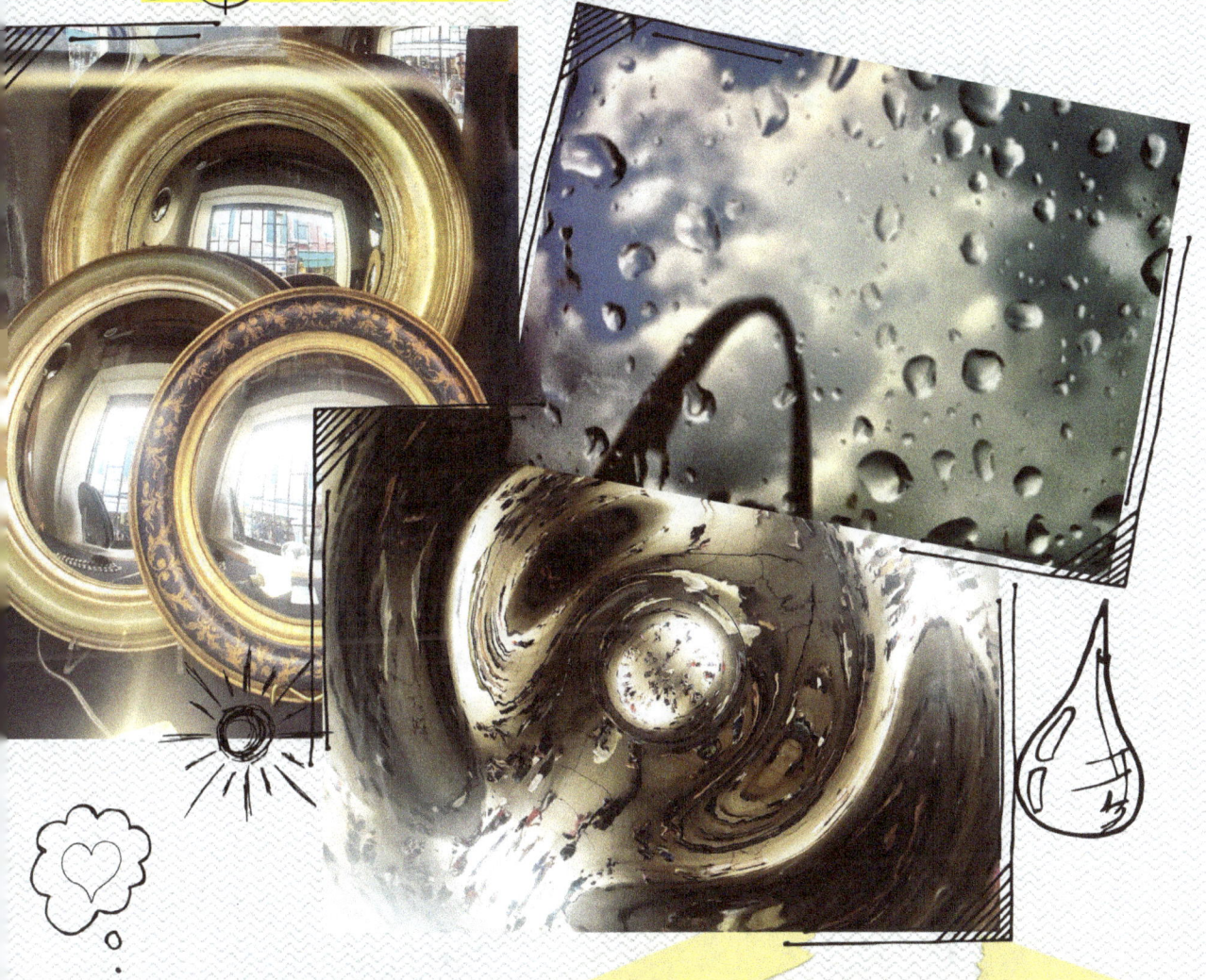

DEPTH OF FEELS:

WAS THIS FUN? CIRCLE

YES OR NO

WHAT WAS IT LIKE BEING A
REFLECTION HUNTER? WHAT
SURPRISED YOU?

WHAT WASN'T EASY? WHY?

F⊙CUS : REFLECTIONS

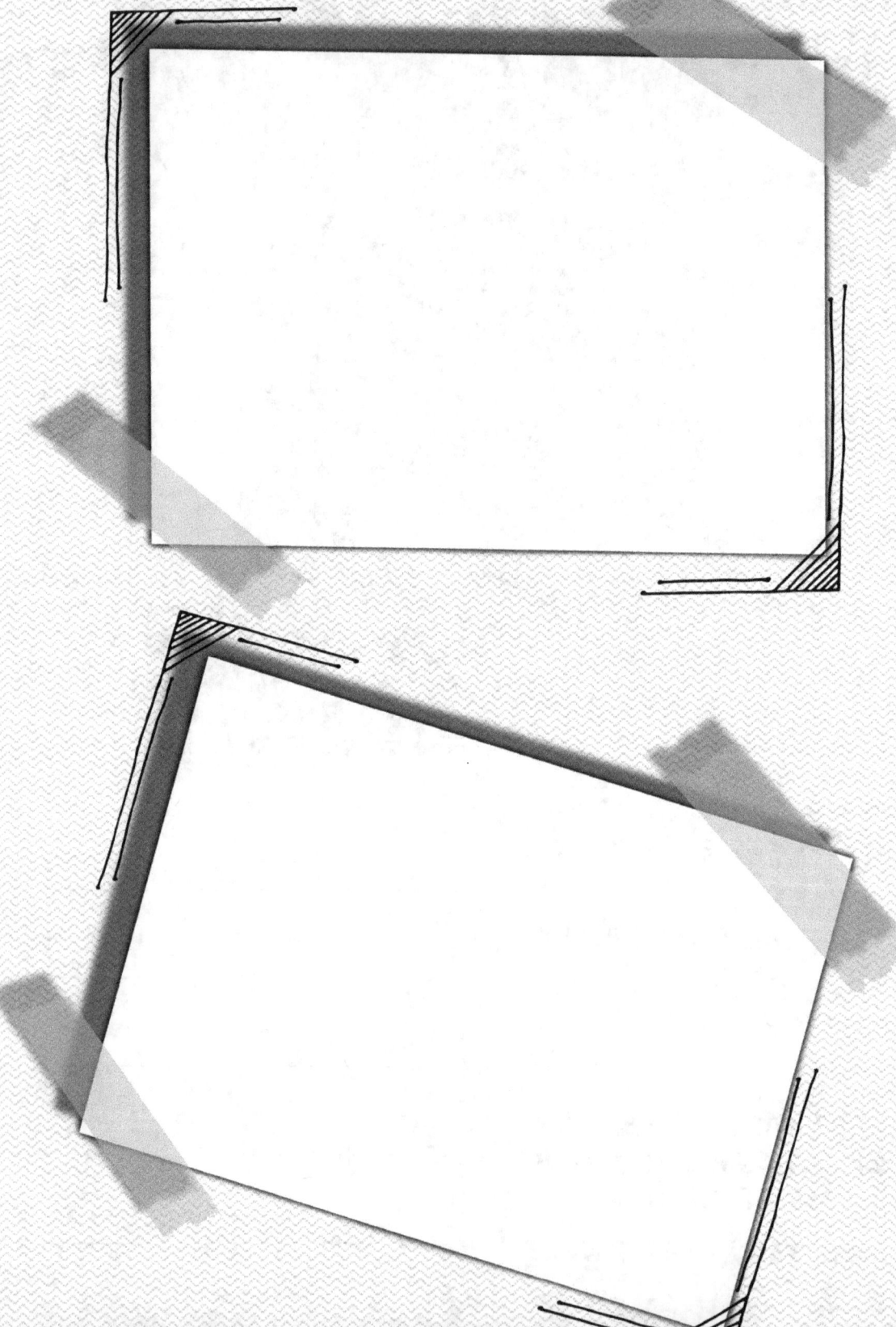

FOCUS : 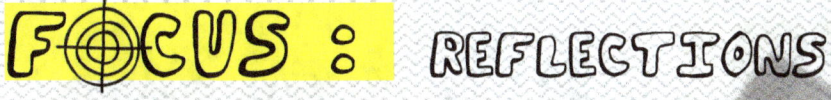 REFLECTIONS

F⊙CUS : PHOTO YOGA, SORTA

WE USE OUR BODIES TO TAKE PICTURES. THINK ABOUT IT, WE USE OUR ARMS, HANDS, FINGERS, EYES, MUSCLES, AND EVEN OUR CORE (THE CENTER OF OUR BODY THAT HOLDS US UP). OUR BODIES BEND AND STRETCH JUST LIKE THEY DO IN YOGA!

SO WHAT IF WE STARTED GETTING CREATIVE WITH OUR BODIES WHEN TAKING PICTURES?

THE COBRA SNAP
LAY ON YOUR BELLY, LIFT YOUR CHEST, AND AIM THE CAMERA!

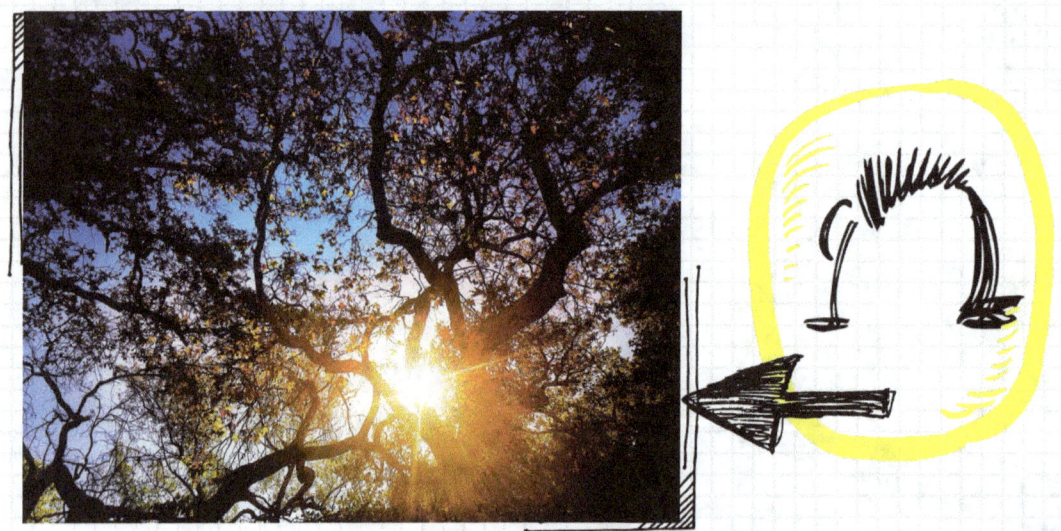

SHAVASANA SNAP
LAY ON YOUR BACK, AIM CAMERA UP TO THE SKY!

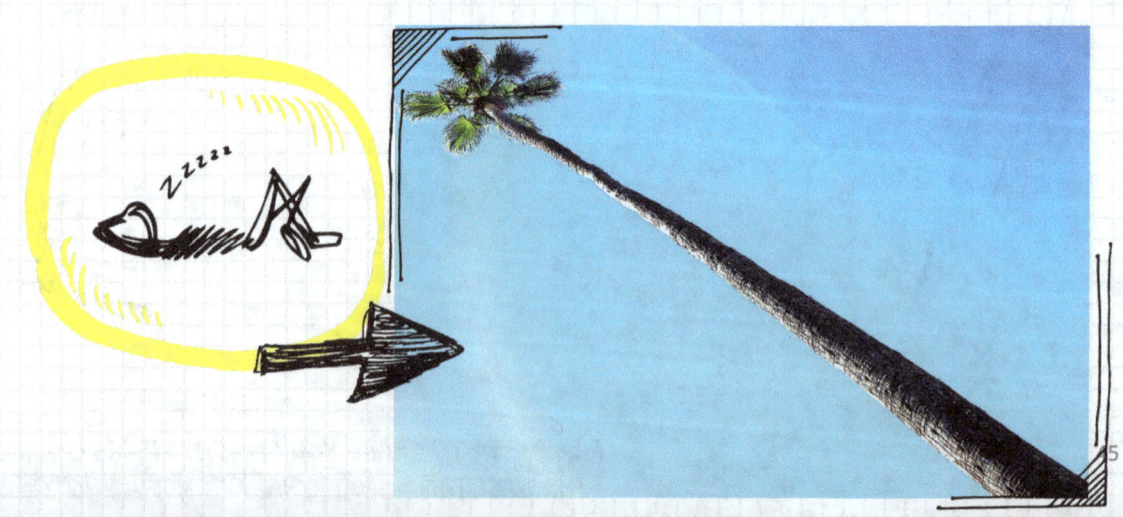

5

FOCUS : PHOTO YOGA, SORTA

TREE POSE SNAP

STAND ON ONE LEG, BRING HANDS TOGETHER AND TAKE THE SNAP!

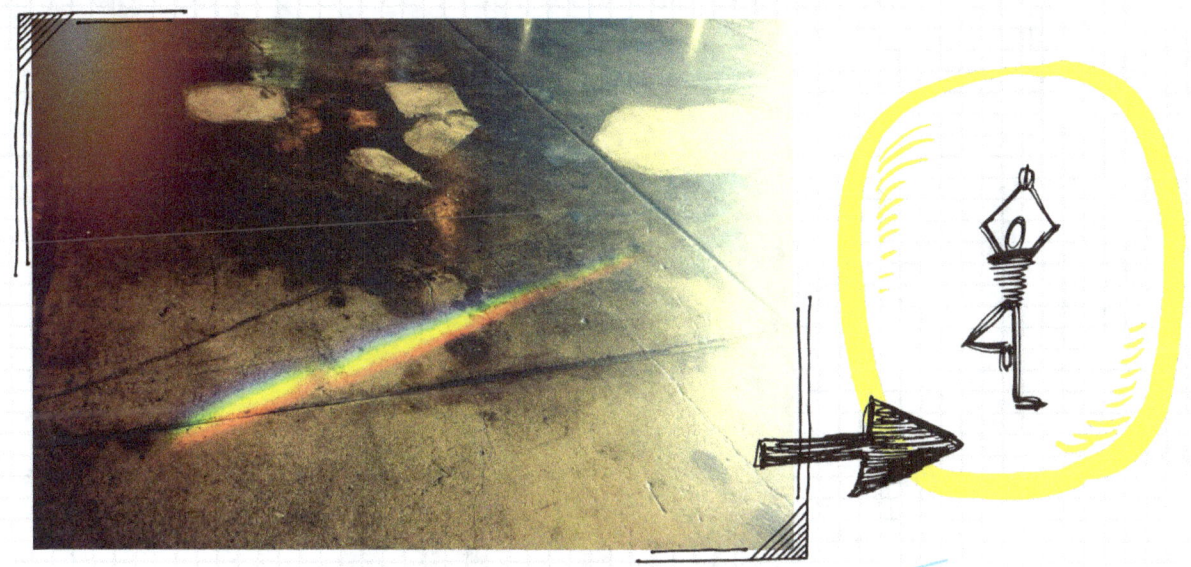

FORWARD BEN SNAP

BEND OVER AND TAKE A PIC LOW TO THE GROUND!

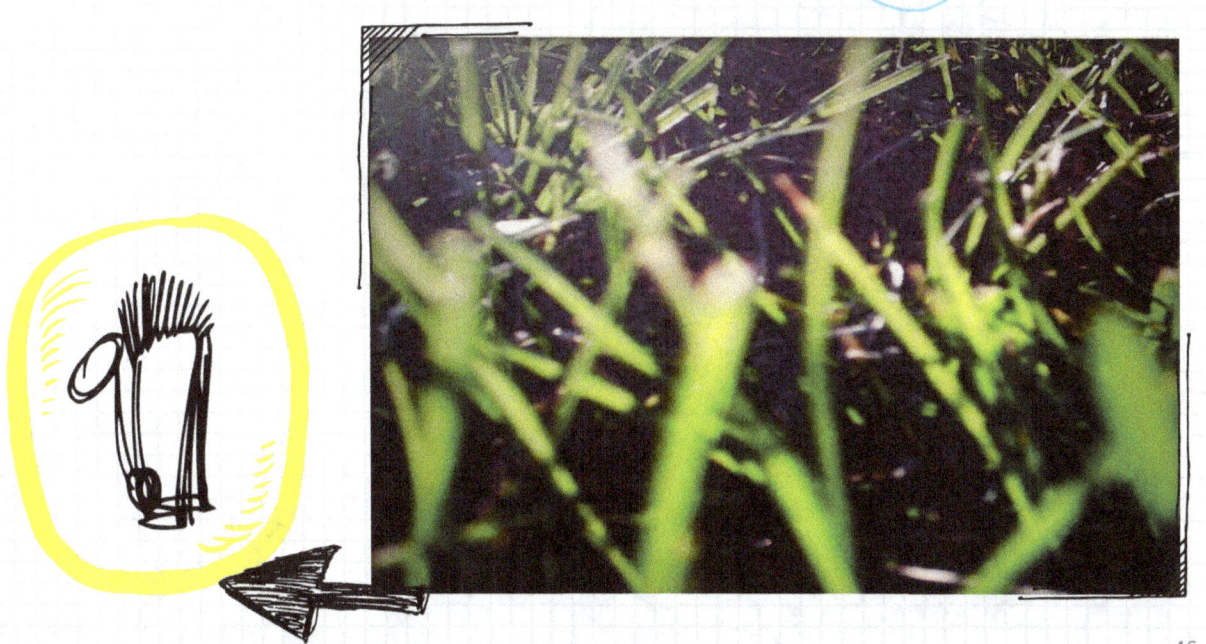

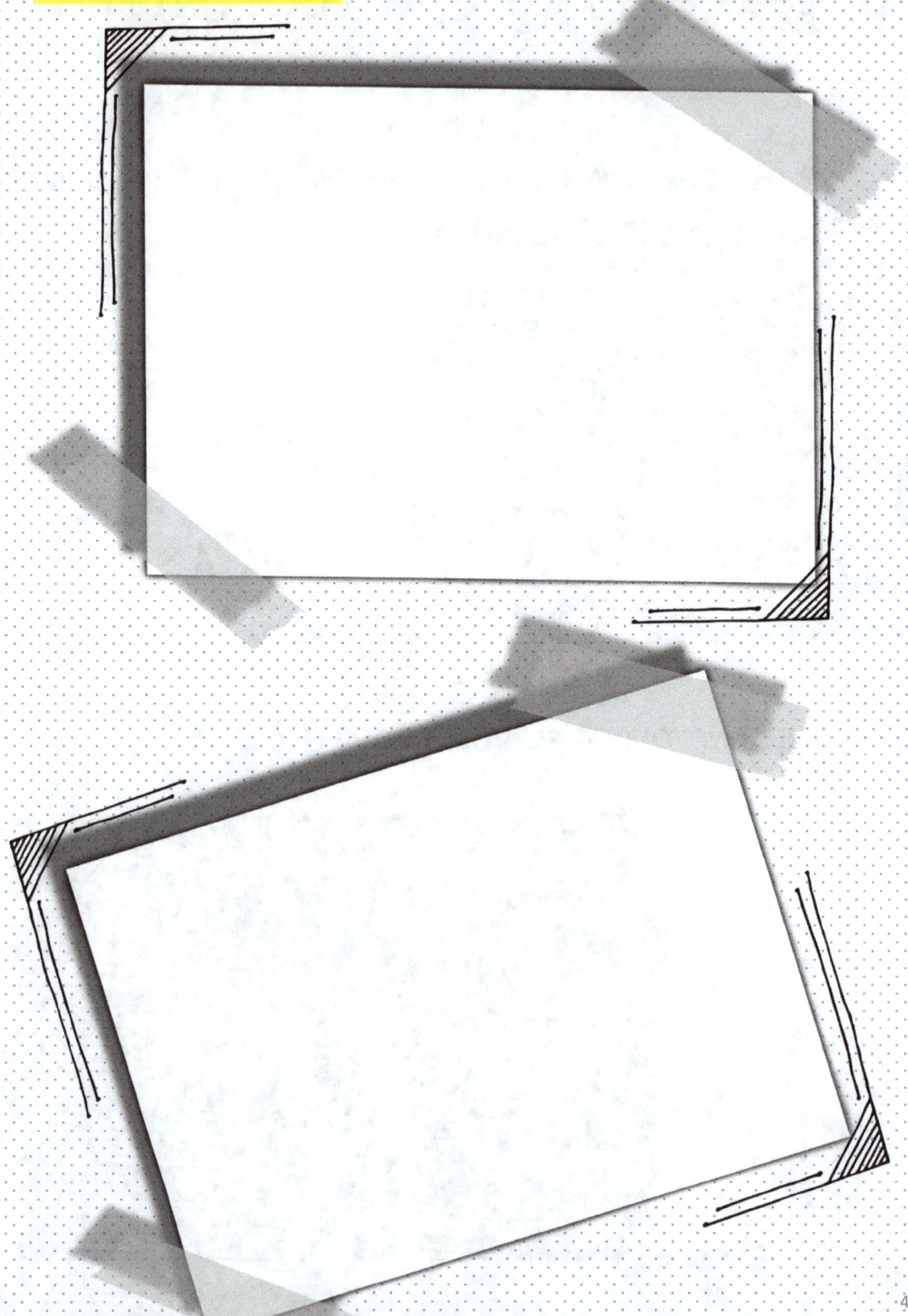

F☉CUS : PHOTO YOGA, SORTA

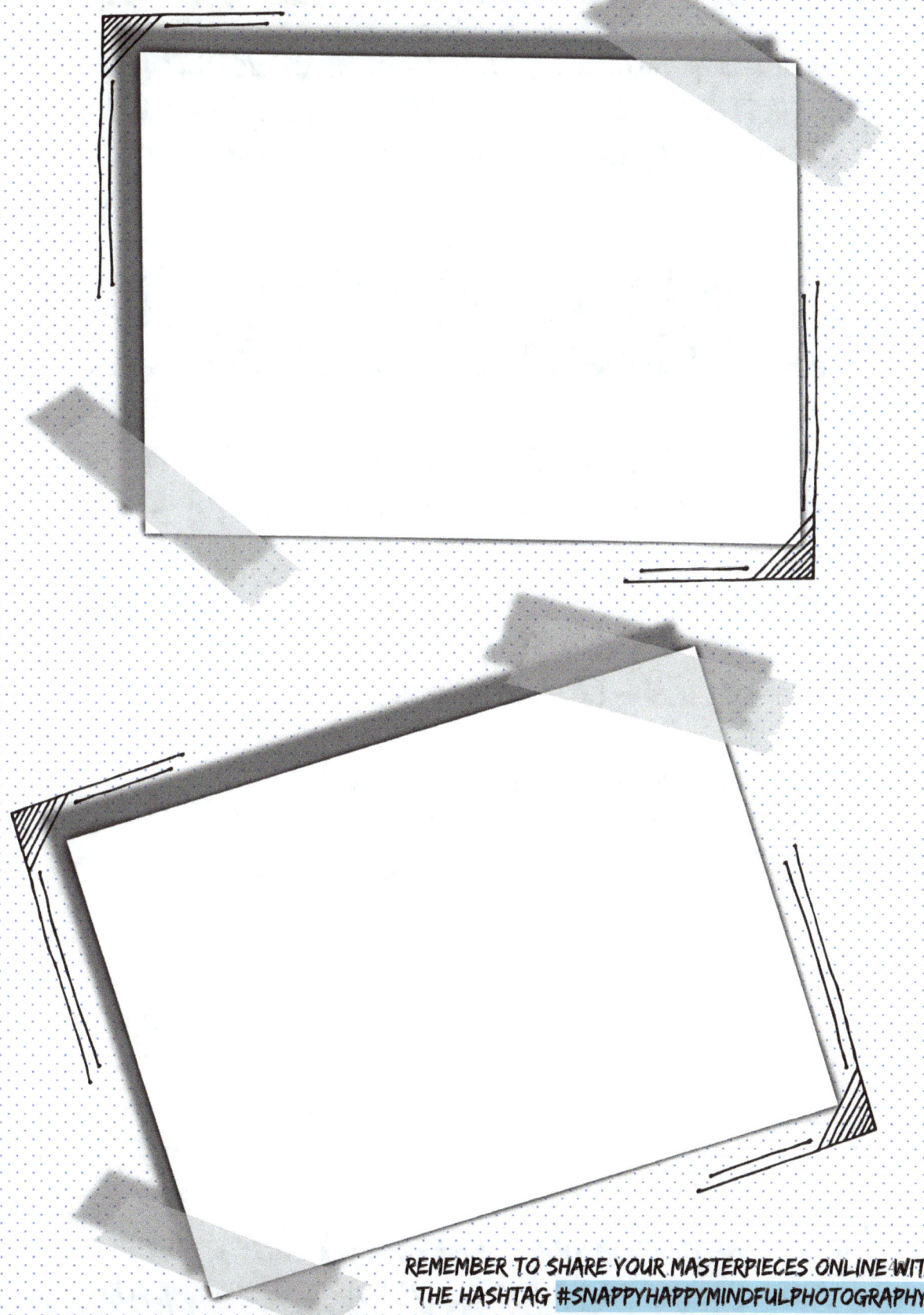

FOCUS : JUMP AROUND

TECHNICALLY, SKILLED PHOTOGRAPHERS WOULD TELL YOU THE FIRST RULE OF PHOTOGRAPHY IS TO STAND STILL SO YOUR PICTURES DON'T BECOME BLURRY OR FUZZY.

YES, SHARP PHOTOS ARE IMPORTANT TO EXPRESS YOUR IMAGE AT ITS MOST CLARITY BUT REMEMBER: MAKING PHOTOS SHOULD BE AS FUN AS THE PHOTO ITSELF.

SO, LET'S MAKE A BLURRY MESS. LET'S MOVE THAT CAMERA ALL OVER THE PLACE! SWIRL THAT CAMERA LIKE A TORNADO!

How to make blurry photos:

☐ Jump when you snap the photo
☐ Spin around and snap the photo
☐ Wiggle your body like a worm and snap the photo
☐ Dance to your favorite song and snap the photo

FUN TIP:

IF YOU HAVE A MANUAL CAMERA, YOU CAN TURN OFF "AUTO FOCUS" SO YOUR PICTURES ARE BLURRY, TOO.

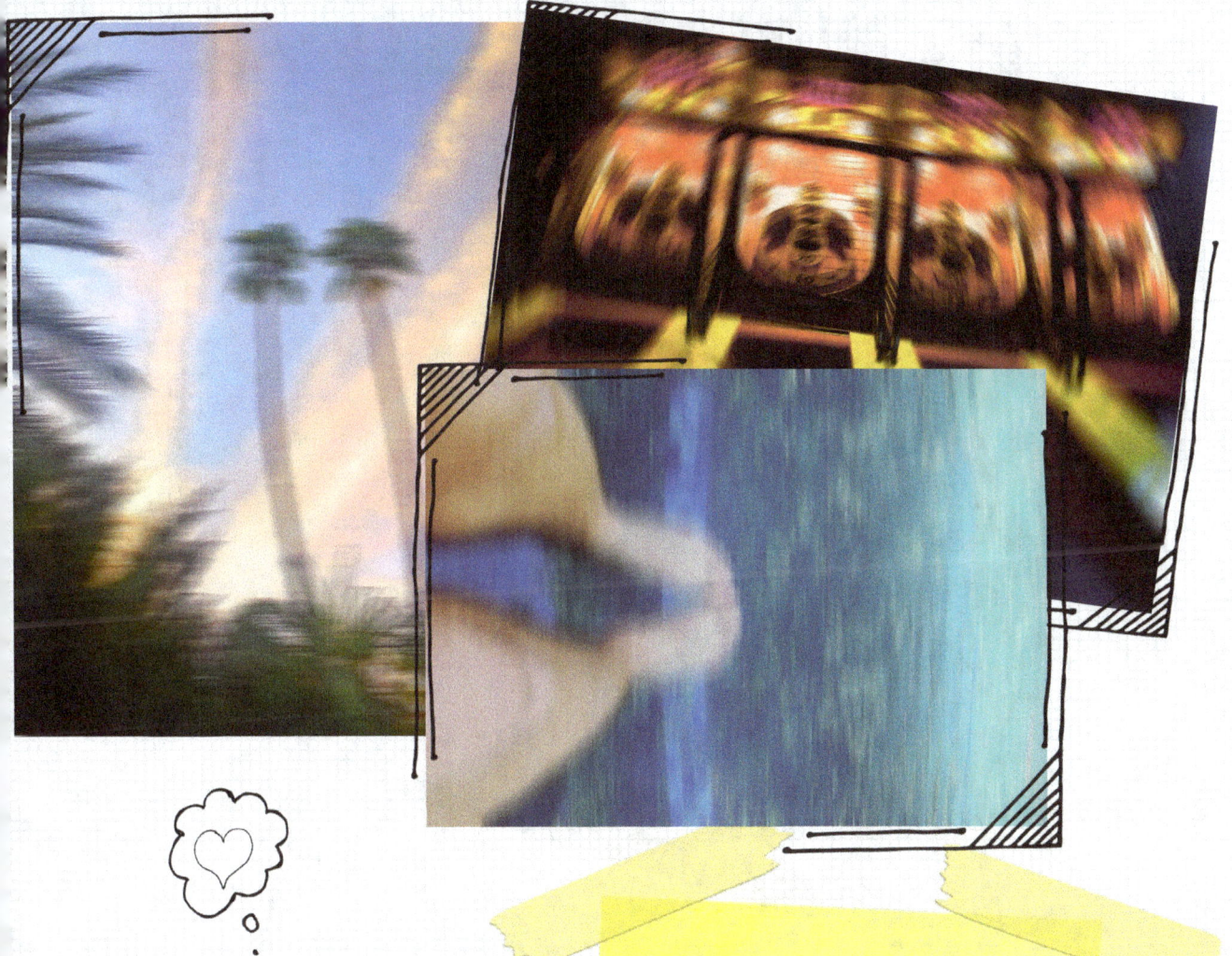

DEPTH OF FEELS:
YES OR NO

WHAT DID IT FEEL LIKE MOVING YOUR BODY WHILE TAKING PICTURES? DID IT FEEL GOOD? WHY? DID IT FEEL WRONG? WHY?

FOCUS : JUMP AROUND

F⊙CUS : JUMP AROUND

THINK ABOUT IT!

PLAY, BEING SILLY, TRYING SOMETHING THAT SEEMS LIKE IT MIGHT TURN OUT WEIRD IS A BIG PART OF MINDFUL PHOTOGRAPHY. WHEN WE ARE MOST CURIOUS ABOUT WHAT WE ARE SEEING AND FEELING WHAT WE ARE EXPLORING, WE ARE MOST PRESENT!

IT'S COOL. THAT PHOTO MIGHT NOT LOOK LIKE HOW YOU THOUGHT IT WOULD, BUT HOW DOES IT FEEL NOW THAT YOU HAVE TRIED SOMETHING — A NEW ANGLE, A DIFFERENT TYPE OF CAMERA? WRITE IT BELOW!

"THE EYE SHOULD LEARN TO LISTEN BEFORE IT LOOKS."

— ROBERT FRANK

FOCUS : HEADS IN THE CLOUDS

CLOUDS ARE LIKE OUR THOUGHTS: THEY MOVE, OFTEN QUICKLY, THOUGH THE SKY ALWAYS CHANGING. IN MINDFULNESS, NOTICING OUR THOUGHTS AND BECOMING AWARE OF HOW THEY ARE AFFECTING OUR MOOD IS EPIC!

JUST LIKE THOUGHTS, CLOUDS SET THE MOOD IN THE SKY. THINK ABOUT IT: DARK GLOOMY ONES MAKE THE SKY FEEL COLD AND GRUMPY. WHITE PUFFY ONES ARE PLAYFUL AND IMAGINATIVE. WISPY ONES ARE LIKE ENERGETIC PAINT STROKE

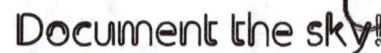

Document the sky!

- Every day, find a spot where you can return to often and snap the sky.

- Don't worry if there are no clouds that moment. Return later to snap another photo, and again that day (maybe five a day at different times).

- Then do it again the next day and for a week!

NOTICE HOW THE SKY IS CONSTANTLY CHANGING — CLOUDS, NO CLOUDS, DIFFERENT CLOUDS, DIFFERENT SHADES OF BLUE.

AS A PHOTOGRAPHER, REMEMBER LIKE HOW CLOUDS ALWAYS CHANGE THE MOMENT YOU ARE CAPTURING IS A MOMENT THAT WILL NEVER BE EXACTLY RECREATED AGAIN!

FOCUS : HEADS IN THE CLOUDS

"Feelings come and go like clouds in a windy sky. Conscious breathing is my anchor." - Thich Nhat Hanh

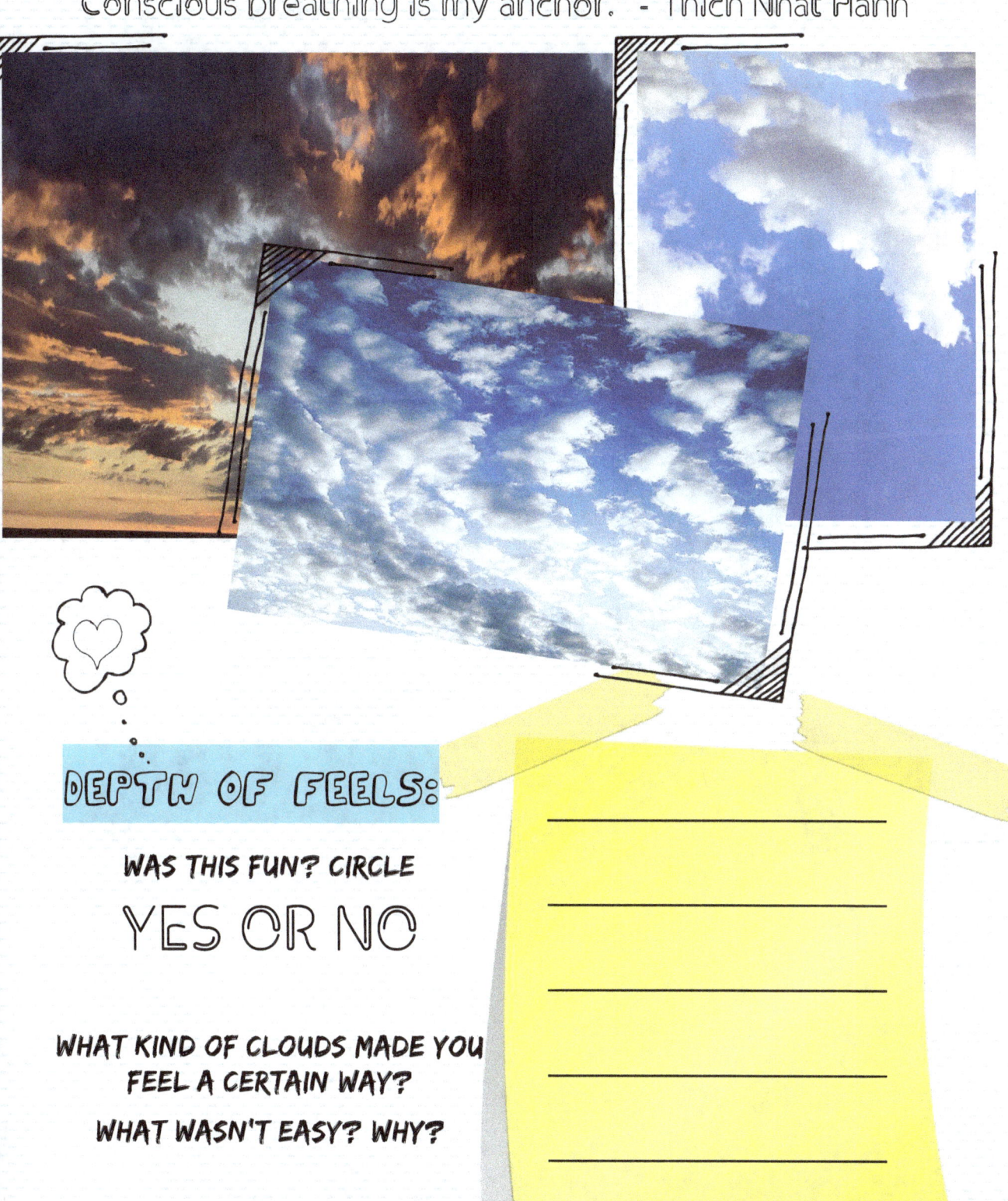

DEPTH OF FEELS:

WAS THIS FUN? CIRCLE

YES OR NO

WHAT KIND OF CLOUDS MADE YOU FEEL A CERTAIN WAY?

WHAT WASN'T EASY? WHY?

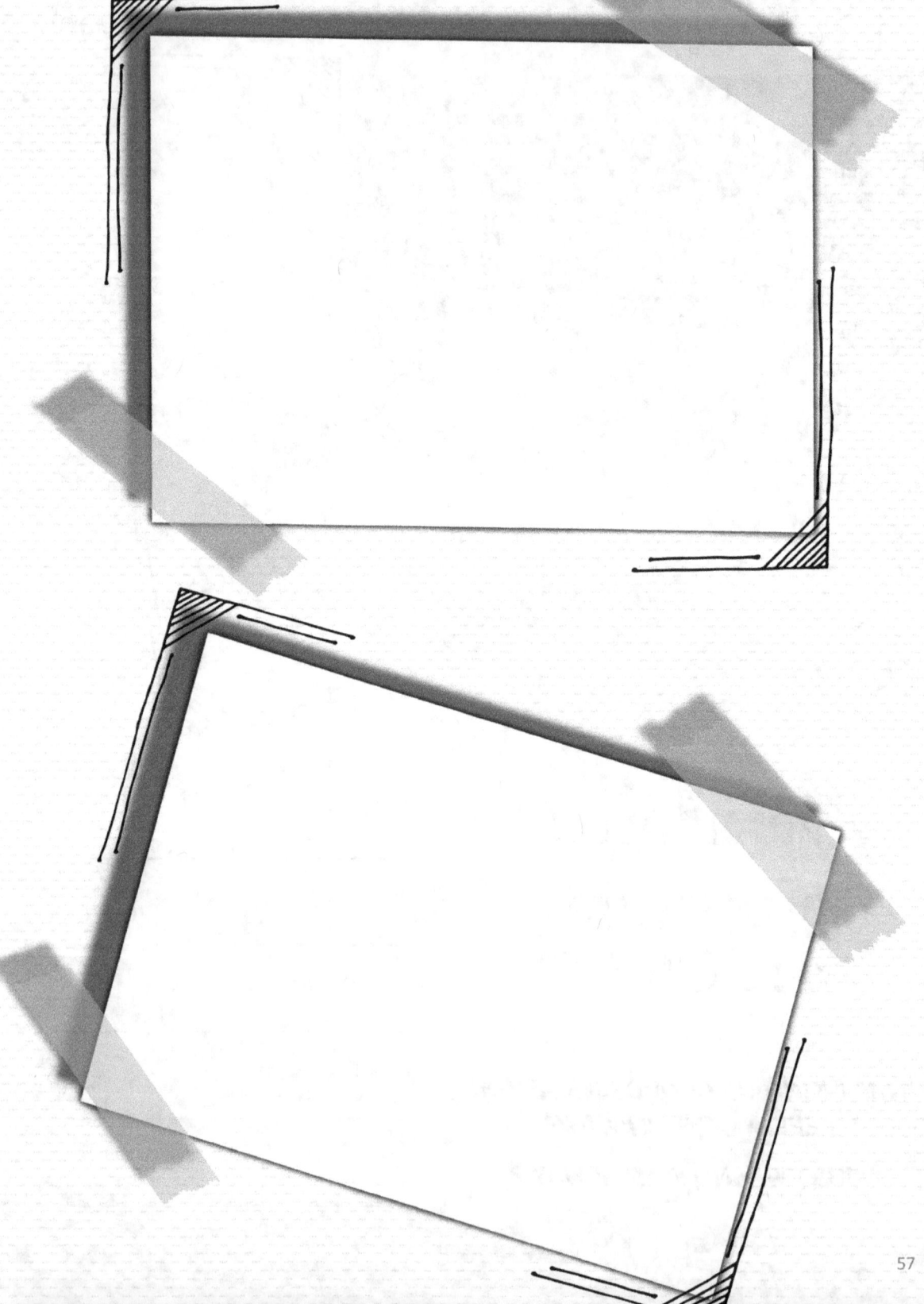

FOCUS : HEAD IN THE CLOUDS

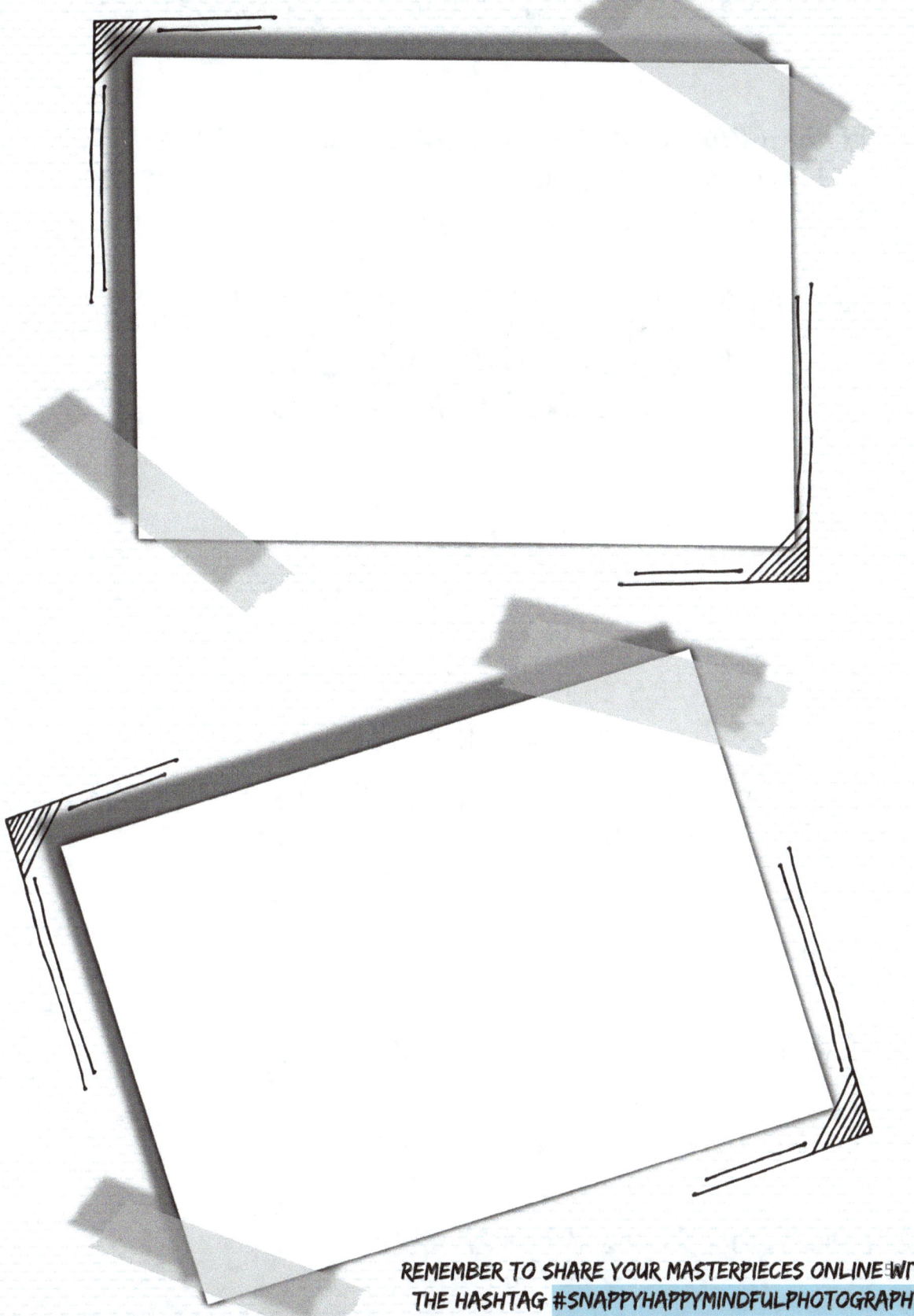

FOCUS : STEP. TURN. SNAP!

YOU'RE GOING TO DO A LITTLE BIT OF FUNNY. IT MIGHT FEEL A LITTLE STRANGE! BUT, YOU KNOW WHAT, THAT'S OK! FEELING WEIRD SOMETIMES INTRODUCES US TO NEW IDEAS!

INSTEAD OF BEING SO FOCUSED ON FINDING SOMETHING TO PHOTOGRAPH, YOU'RE GOING TO LET YOUR BODY FIND IT FOR YOU!

How it works:

1. You're going to close your eyes.
2. Take one step in any direct.
3. Turn in one direction.
4. Now, open your eyes and whatever is in front of you, snap a picture!

REPEAT!

REPEAT!

REPEAT!

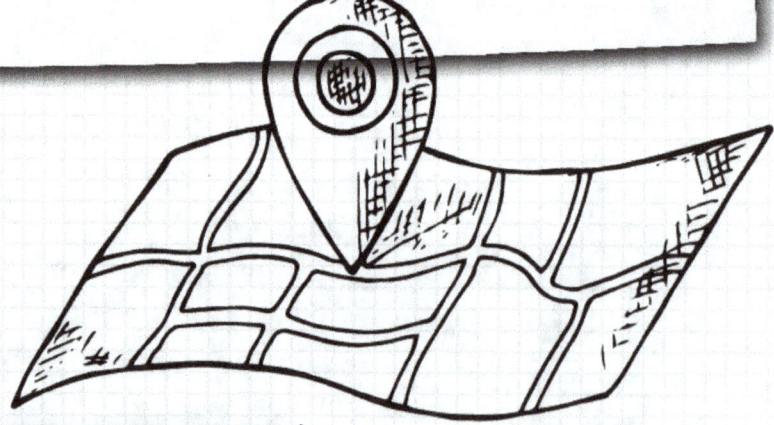

GET DIZZY, GET SILLY. GET SNAP HAPPY!

FOCUS : STEP. TURN. SNAP!

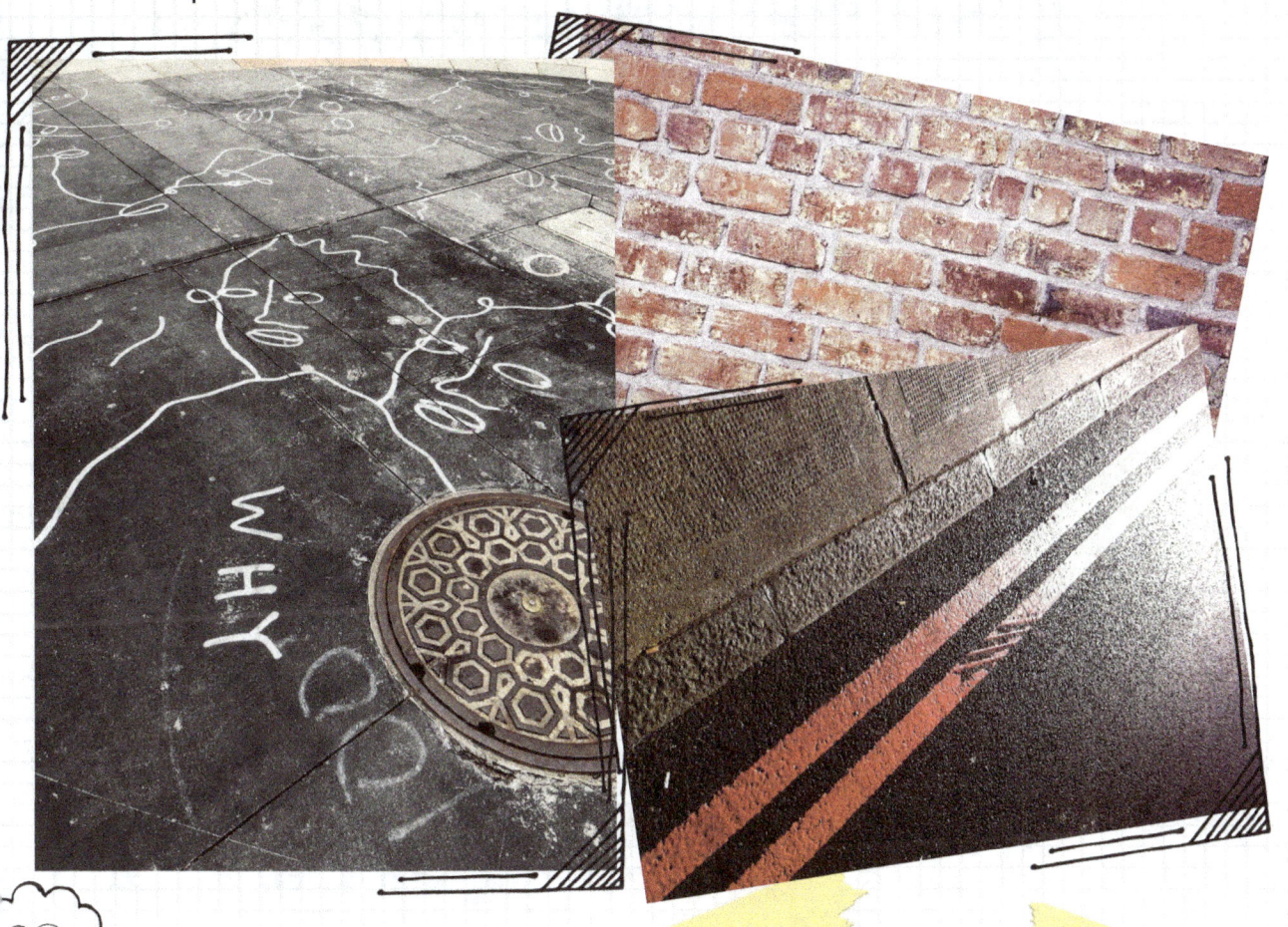

DEPTH OF FEELS:

WAS THIS FUN? CIRCLE

YES OR NO

WHAT DID IT FEEL LIKE NOT
KNOWING WHAT PICTURE YOU'D

TAKE AFTER SPINNING?

WHAT WASN'T EASY? WHY?

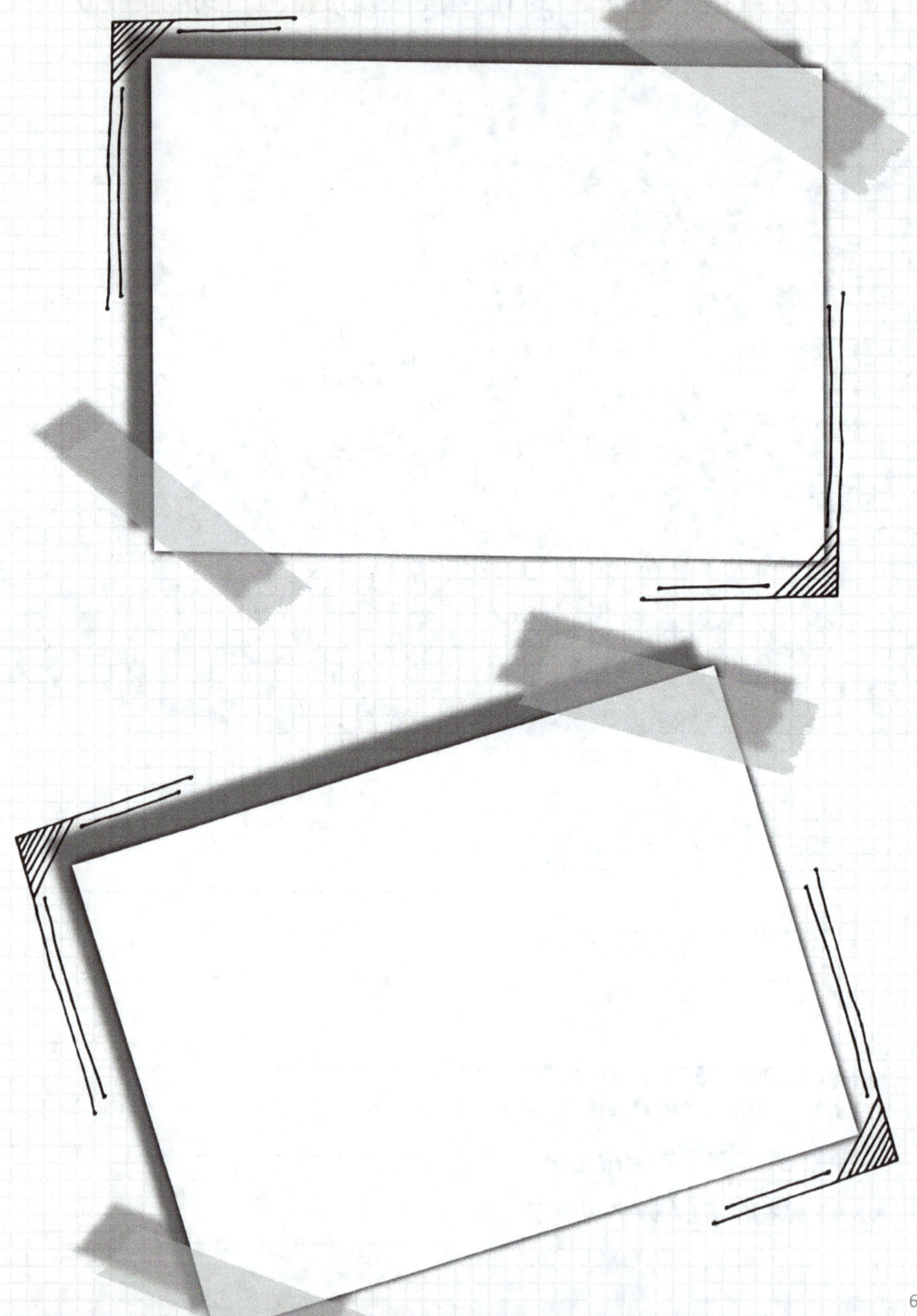

F⊙CUS : STEP. SPIN. SNAP!

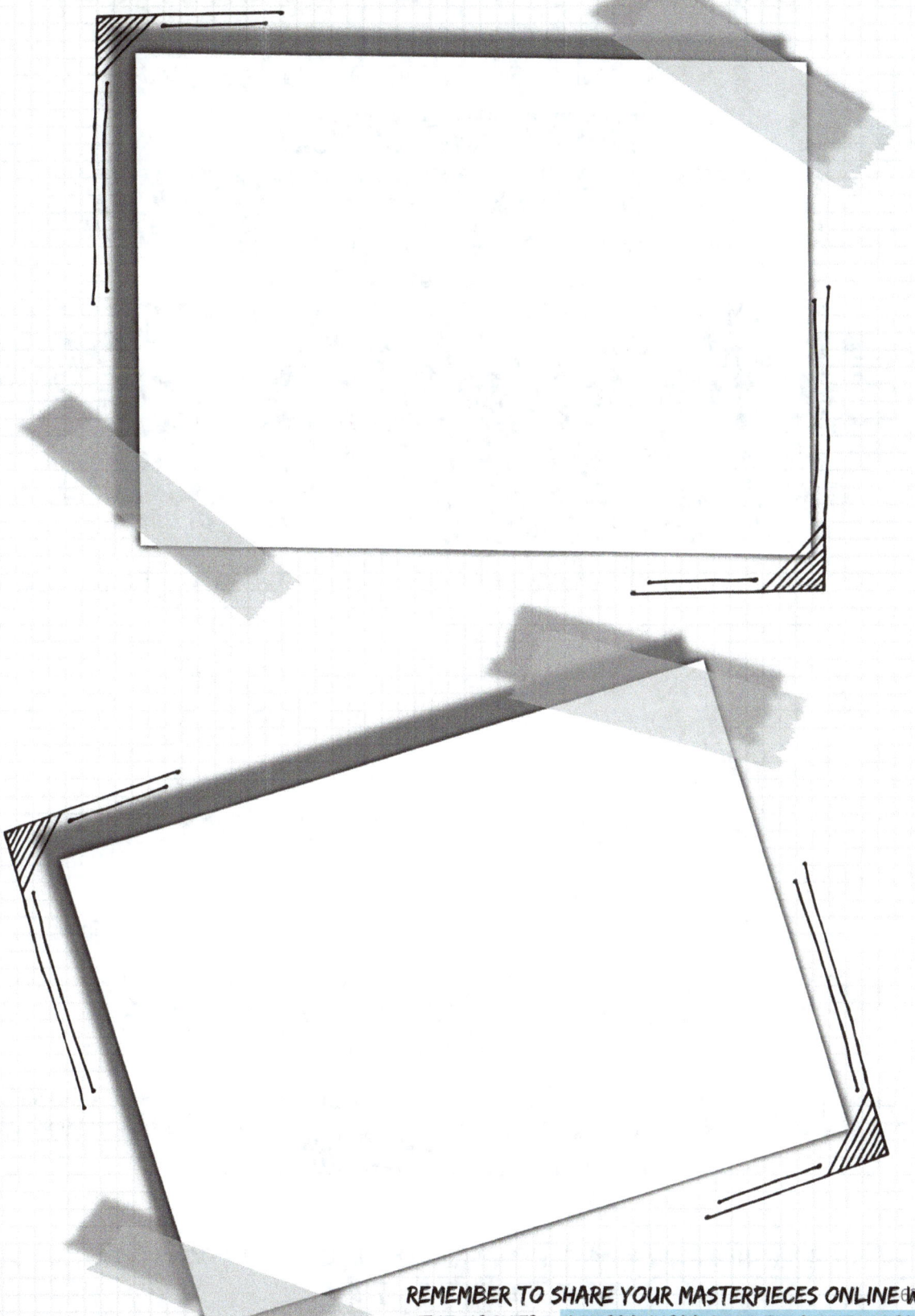

FOCUS : ONE PIC A DAY

You will only take one picture a day.

YUP. YOU READ THAT RIGHT.

OOOOOO, ARE YOU GETTING UNCOMFORTABLE WITH THAT ASSIGNMENT? KNOWING THAT YOU ONLY GET ONE SHOT A DAY IS PRETTY MUCH LIKE, HUH?! BUT...

BACK IN THE OLDEN DAYS (DON'T TELL YOUR PARENTS I CALLED THESE THE OLDEN DAYS), YOU USED TO ONLY HAVE FILM AND THERE WERE LIMITED AMOUNTS OF PICTURES ON THAT FILM. SOMETIMES 24 PICTURES, SOMETIMES, 36. AND DEVELOPING THAT FILM WAS KINDA EXPENSIVE SO YOU WERE VERY MINDFUL OF WHAT YOU TOOK PICTURES OF AND HOW YOU TOOK THE PICTURES.

So basically, you're going into a time machine of mindfulness!

What can this skill teach you?

- To be purposeful with what you want to photograph
- To think of the time of day to photograph
- To not have regrets once you take the picture.

ARE YOU NOT SURE ABOUT THIS? GOOD. IT'S GOOD TO BE A LITTLE BIT NERVOUS. ASK YOURSELF WHY?

AND IF YOU'RE LIKE, "COOL. LET'S DO THIS!" ASK YOURSELF, WHY AM I SO COMFORABLE WITH THIS?

BEING A PICTURE MAKER INVOLVES ASKING YOURSELF QUESTIONS AS MUCH AS IT IS THE PICTURE ITSELF.

FOCUS : ONE PIC A DAY

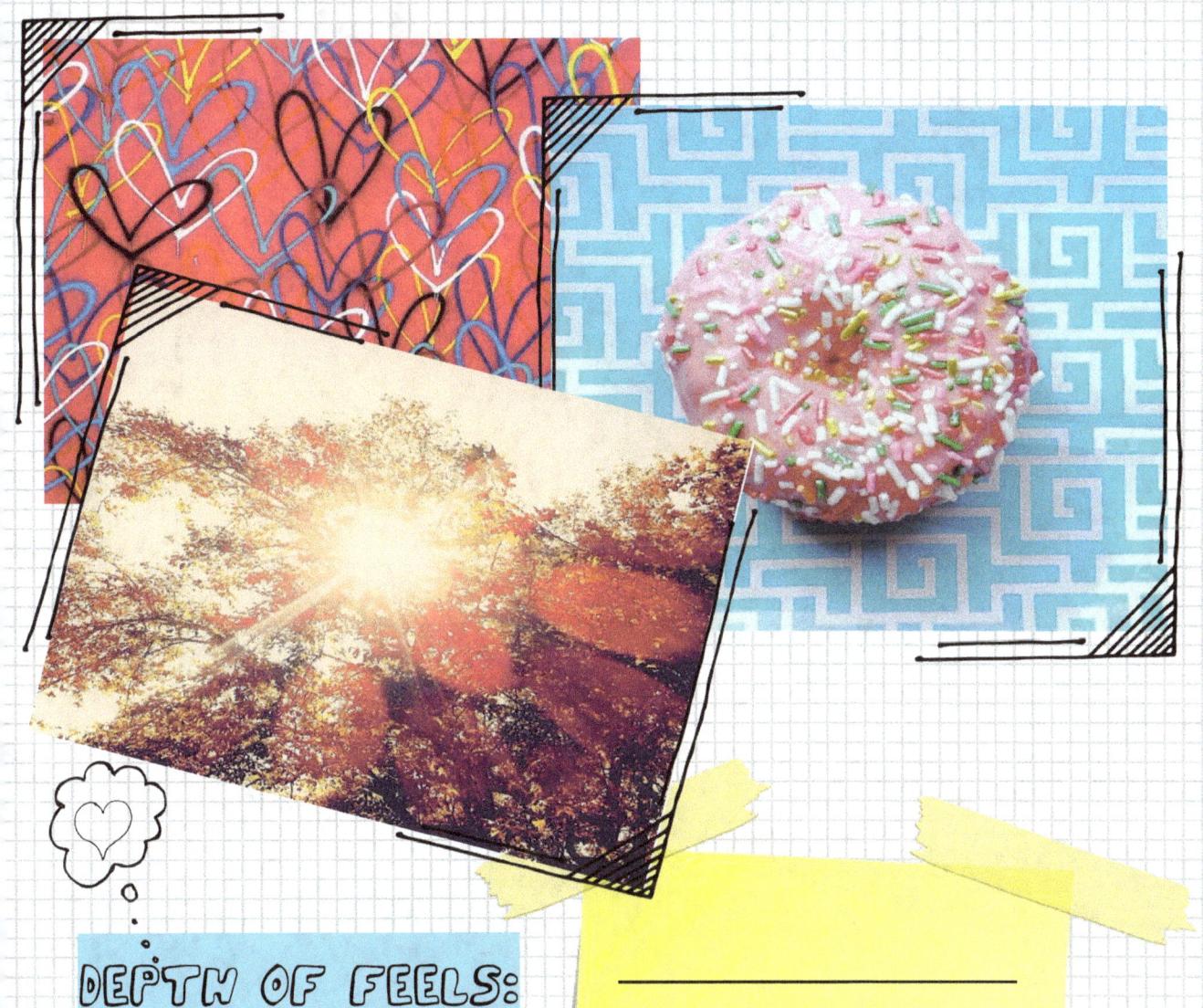

DEPTH OF FEELS:

WAS THIS FUN? CIRCLE

YES OR NO

WHAT WAS EASY ABOUT THIS
ADVENTURE? HOW COME?

WHAT WASN'T EASY? WHY?

F⊙CUS : ONE PIC A DAY

REMEMBER TO SHARE YOUR MASTERPIECES ONLINE WITH THE HASHTAG #SNAPPYHAPPYMINDFULPHOTOGRAPHY

"PATIENCE IS THE ESSENCE OF CLICKING GREAT PHOTOGRAPHS!"

— ABHIJEET SAWANT

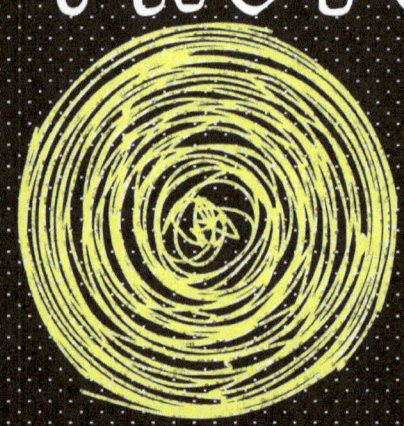

THINK ABOUT IT

USE THIS PAGE IN ANY WAY YOU'D LIKE, BUT CAN WE MAKE A SUGGESTION? MAYBE WRITE DOWN SOME NOTES ABOUT HOW YOU ARE FEELING AND LEARNING SOME OF THESE WAYS TO EXPLORE WITH THE CAMERA. ARE YOU HAVING FUN? WHY OR WHY NOT? ARE YOU FEELING DIFFERENT THAN WHEN YOU STARTED BEFORE THIS

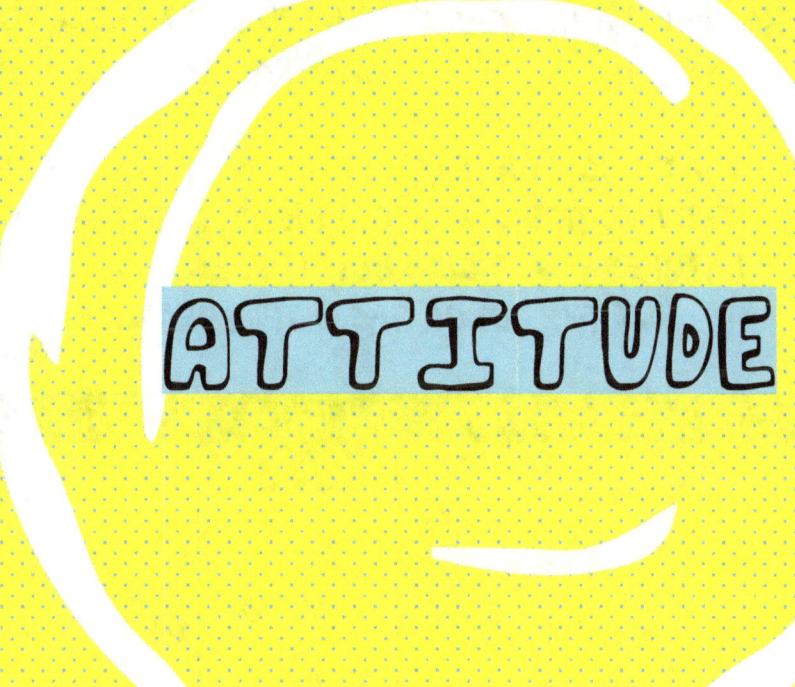

ATTITUDE

F⊙CUS : FEEL THE LIGHT

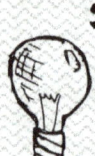
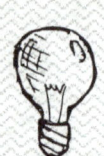

SOMETIMES WE TAKE FOR GRANTED THE SIMPLEST THINGS: FOR EXAMPLE, LIGHT. ARE EYES NEED IT TO SEE, AND SO DOES A CAMERA!

ISO – THAT'S HOW CAMERA'S SENSITIVITY CREATE PICTURES – THE HIGHER THE ISO, THE LOWER THE LIGHT. LIGHT ALSO HAS DIFFERENT TEMPERATURES – NOT LIKE HOW IT FEELS SO HOT IN THE SUMMER, BUT THE COLOR HAS A TEMPERATURE. MAGIC!

WE'VE GOT SO MANY TYPES OF LIGHT – LET'S SEE HOW THAT LIGHT LOOKS!

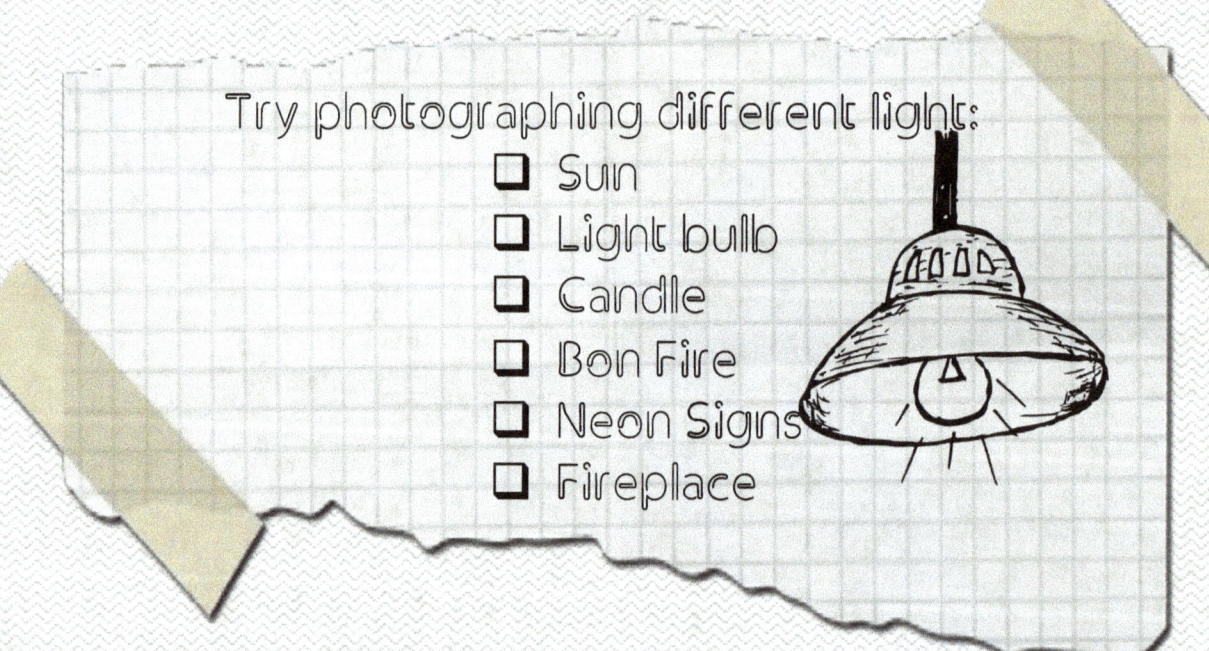

Try photographing different light:
- ☐ Sun
- ☐ Light bulb
- ☐ Candle
- ☐ Bon Fire
- ☐ Neon Signs
- ☐ Fireplace

SOME QUESTIONS TO PONDER:

DOES THE CAMERA MAKE THE LIGHT LOOK DIFFERENT THAN OUR EYES? WHAT KIND OF FEELINGS DO YOU GET FROM DIFFERENT KIND OF LIGHT? WHICH DO YOU PREFER? WHY?

FIND DIFFERENT SOURCES THAT LIGHT UP YOUR LIFE!

FOCUS : FEEL THE LIGHT

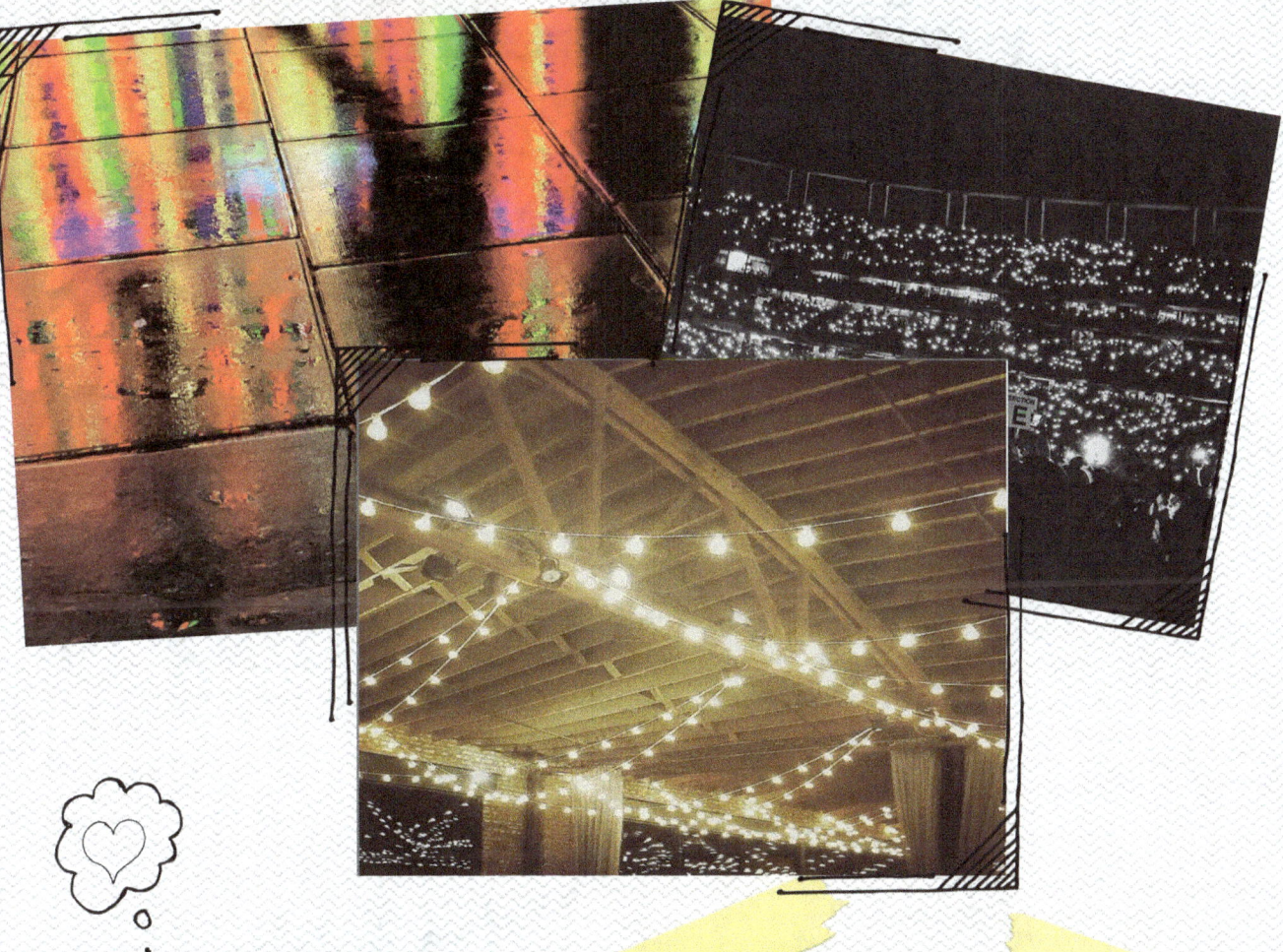

DEPTH OF FEELS:

WAS THIS FUN? CIRCLE

YES OR NO

WHAT WAS IT LIKE BEING A LIGHT HUNTER?

WHAT SURPRISED YOU?

WHAT WASN'T EASY? WHY?

FOCUS : FEEL THE LIGHT

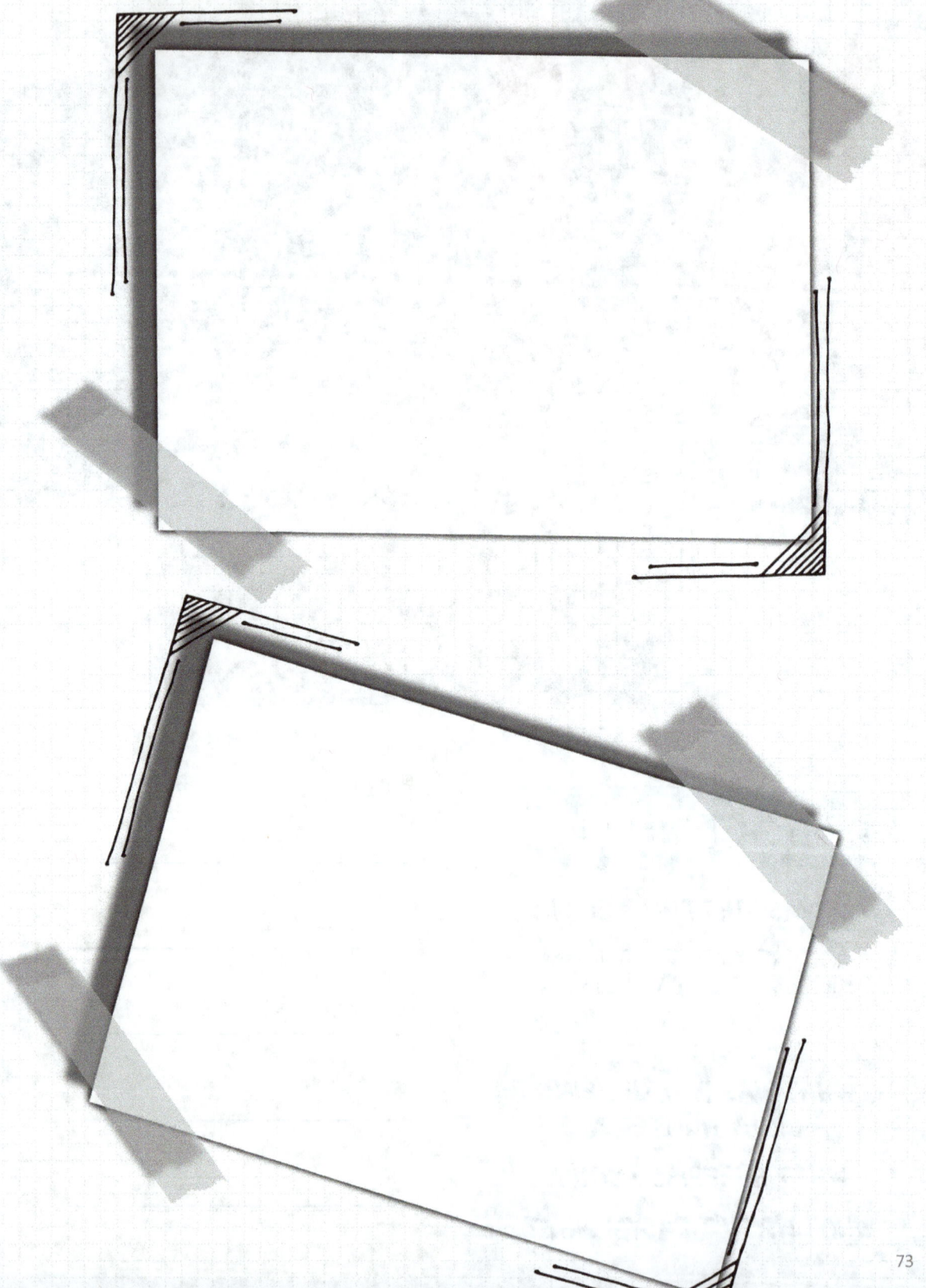

FOCUS : FEEL THE LIGHT

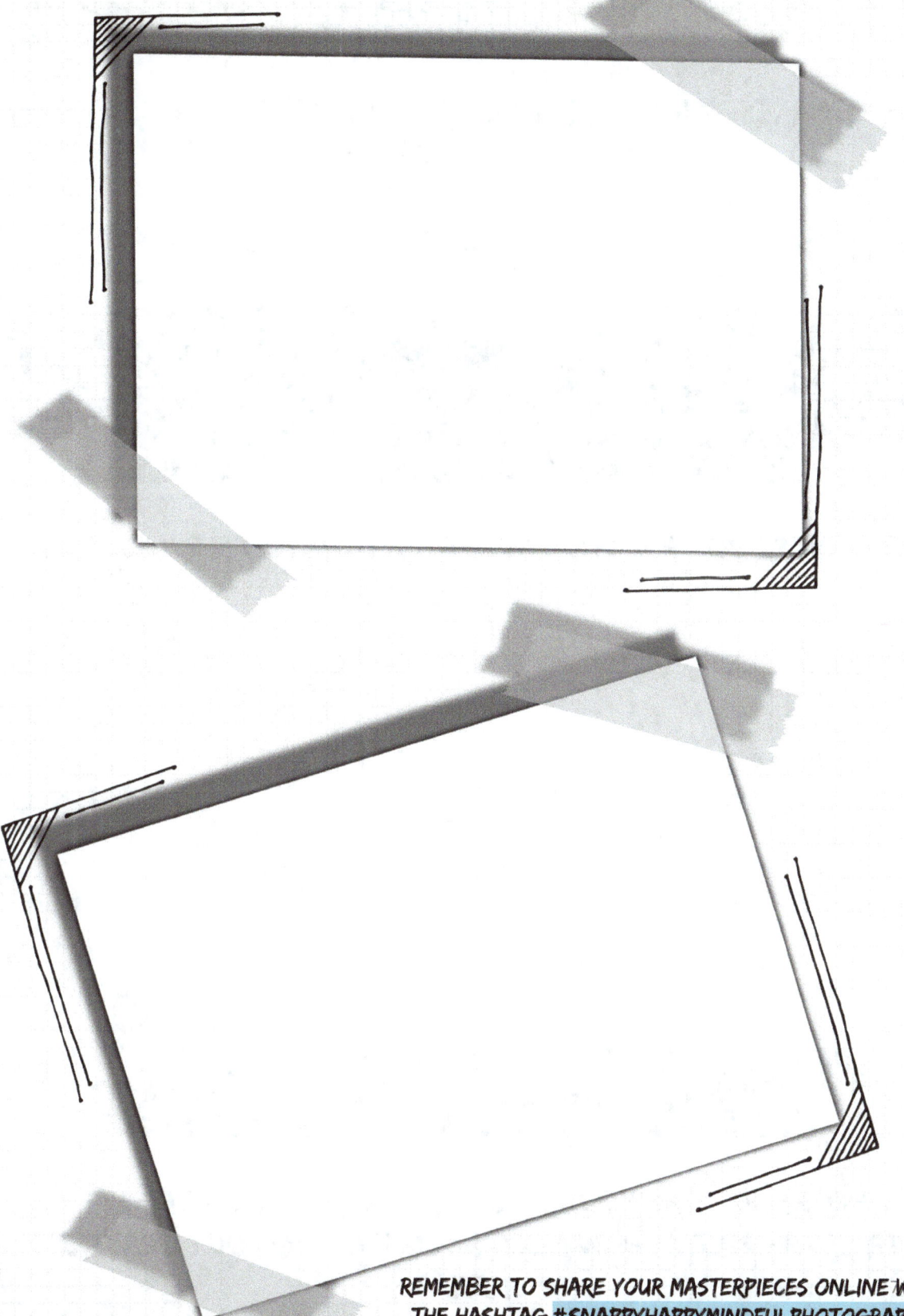

FOCUS : FEEL THE LIGHT

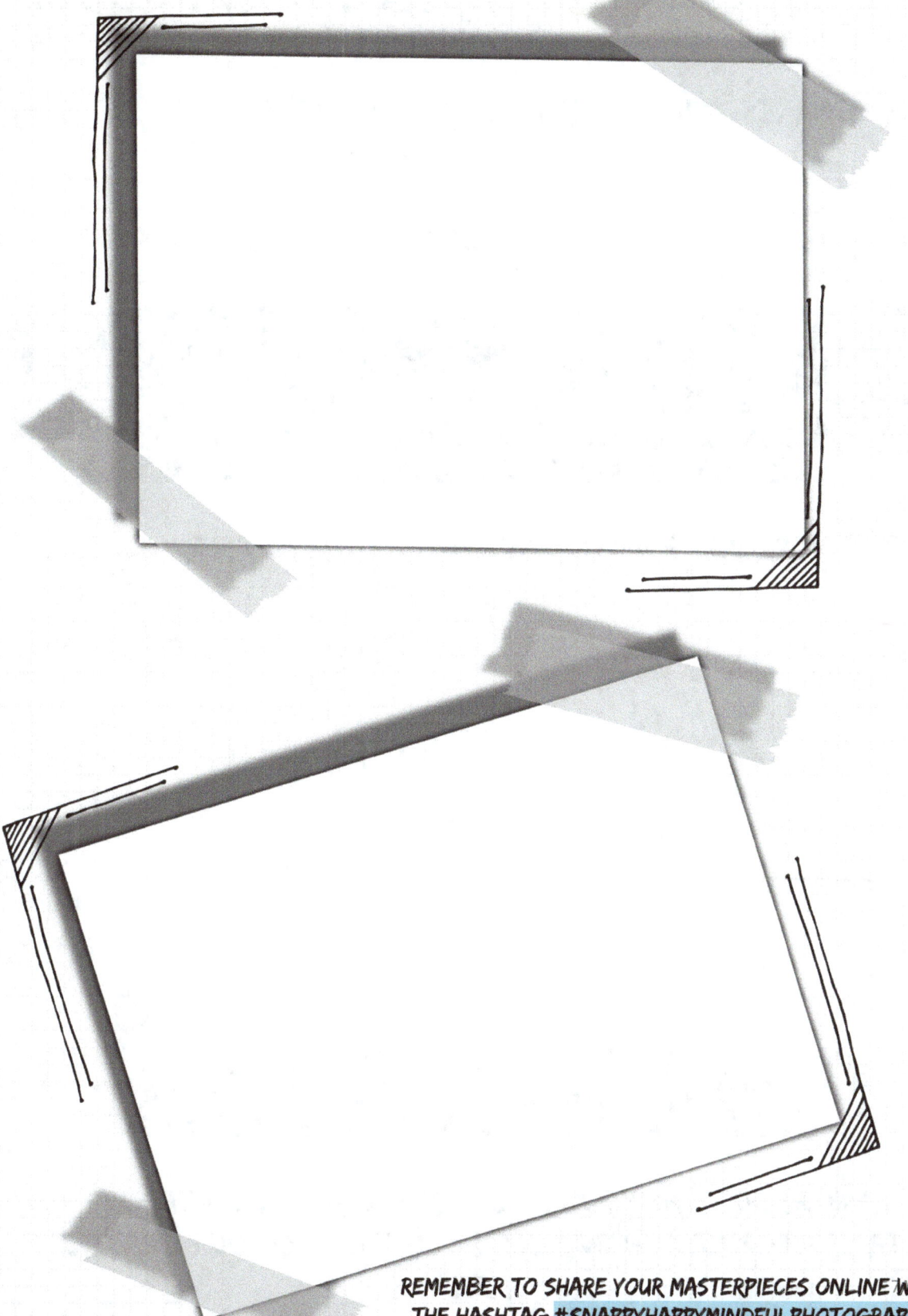

FOCUS : GRATITUDE ATTITUDE

WHAT MAKES YOUR HEART BURST? WELL, NOT LITERALLY. THAT WOULD BE KINDA MESSY.

SO WHAT ARE YOU THANKFUL FOR IN YOUR LIFE?

SCIENTIFIC STUDIES HAVE FOUND THAT PRACTICING GRATITUDE OFTEN CAN BE GOOD FOR YOUR BODY AND MIND! IT'S LIKE A FREE VITAMIN YOU DON'T HAVE TO GUZZLE DOWN WITH WATER! WOWZA. IT EVEN MAKES YOUR BRAIN SMARTER! MAGIC!

THE MORE YOU PRACTICE GRATITUDE, THE BETTER YOU FEEL!

You are going to explore what makes you grateful.

- capture feelings using closeup, textures, subjects you choose or
- even abstract colors that are symbolic for what you feel grateful for right now!

YOUR GOAL IS TO FIND THE THINGS IN YOUR LIFE YOU ARE GRATEFUL FOR AND SNAP THEM TO HONOR THEM.

THINK ABOUT WHY YOU ARE GRATEFUL FOR THEM BEFORE YOU TAKE THE PHOTO. HOW DOES DOCUMENTING YOUR GRATITUDE FEEL?

F⊙CUS : GRATITUDE ATTITUDE

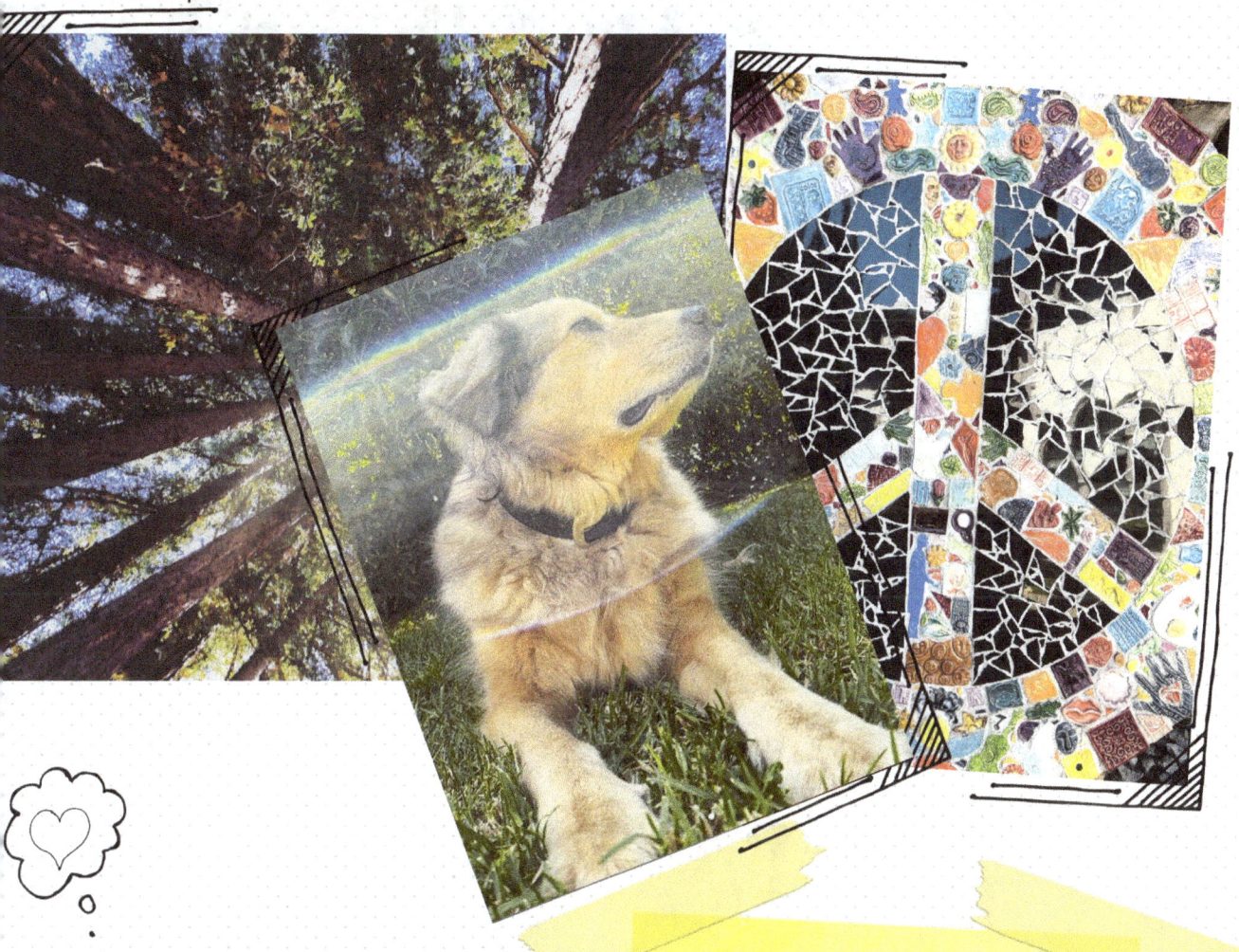

DEPTH OF FEELS:

WAS THIS FUN? CIRCLE

YES OR NO

WHAT DOES SNAPPING GRATITUDE
MAKE YOU FEEL LIKE?

WHAT WASN'T EASY? WHY?

FOCUS : GRATITUDE ATTITUDE

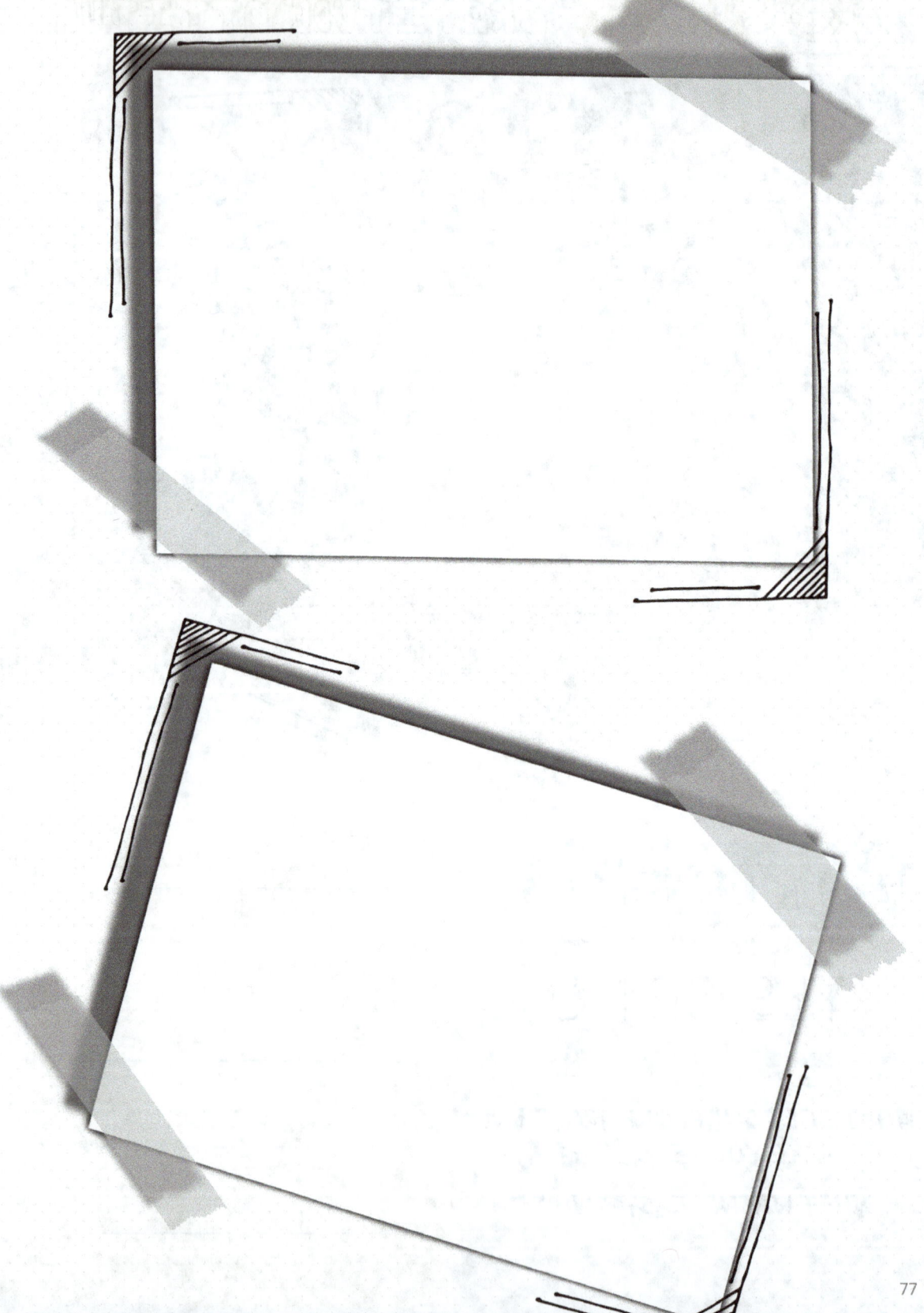

FOCUS : 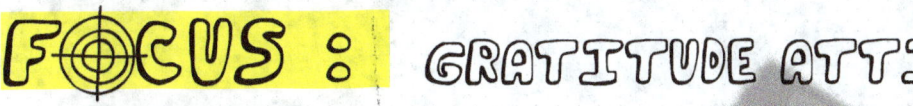 GRATITUDE ATTITUDE

"LOSE THE EGO AND LET THE PHOTOGRAPH FIND YOU."

— ELI REED

THINK ABOUT IT!

LOOK BACK AT SOME OF THE PHOTOS YOU'VE TAKEN. WHICH ARE YOUR FAVORITES AND WHY?

KINDA HARD TO PICK? NO PROBLEM. PICK AS MANY AS YOU LIKE. WHAT MAKES THEM SPECIAL FOR YOU? HOW CAN YOU TAKE PHOTOS THAT MAKE YOU FEEL PROUD?

FOCUS : FEEL IT OUT!

HI. HOW ARE YOU? GOOD? MEH? BLAH? YAY? BOO? HA? WHAT ARE YOU FEELING AT THIS EXACT MOMENT? MAYBE YOU ARE JUST CONTENT?

NOW, HOW CAN YOU PHOTOGRAPH THAT FEELING USING TEXTURES?

TEXTURES IN PHOTOGRAPHY CAN BE CAPTURED IN CLOSE-UPS OF DETAIL ON SURFACES FOUND ALL OVER THE PLACE: HOME, NATURE, STREETS, AND EVEN ON YOU! THINK OF THE ROUGH BARK ON A TREE TRUNK, THE LITTLE BUMPS ON THE STREET, AND THE RIPPLES OF WATER AND SNAP THEM CLOSE UP! IT'S LIKE ABSTRACT ART: THE DESIGN AND LOOK INSPIRES FEELING AND MEANING.

TODAY GO OUT AND DOCUMENT YOUR FEELING IN TEXTURES!

Document these feelings in textures:

- ☐ Happy
- ☐ Excited
- ☐ Sad
- ☐ Mysterious
- ☐ Silly
- ☐ Thoughtful

SOME TIPS:

USE BRIGHT, CLEAR LIGHT TO MAKE TEXTURES DEFINED OR USE SHADOWS ON TEXTURE TO MAKE THEM MYSTERIOUS!

EXAMPLE OF TEXTURE: SOFT, WARM GRASS COULD MEAN HAPPY!

F⊙CUS : FEEL IT OUT!

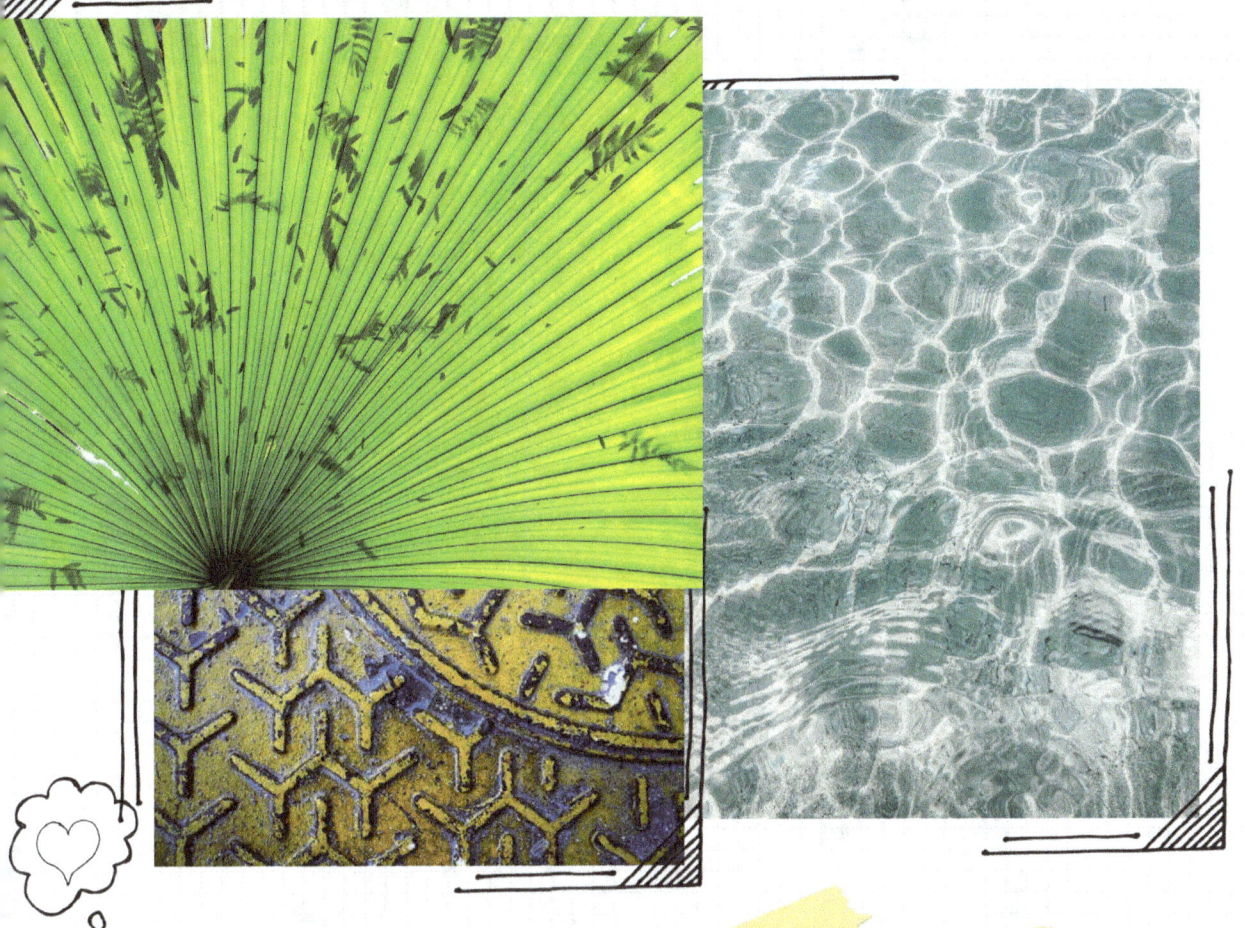

DEPTH OF FEELS:

WAS THIS FUN? CIRCLE

YES OR NO

DID SOME PHOTOS YOU TOOK MAKE YOU FEEL MORE THAN ONE FEELING? WHICH FEELINGS?

WHAT WASN'T EASY? WHY?

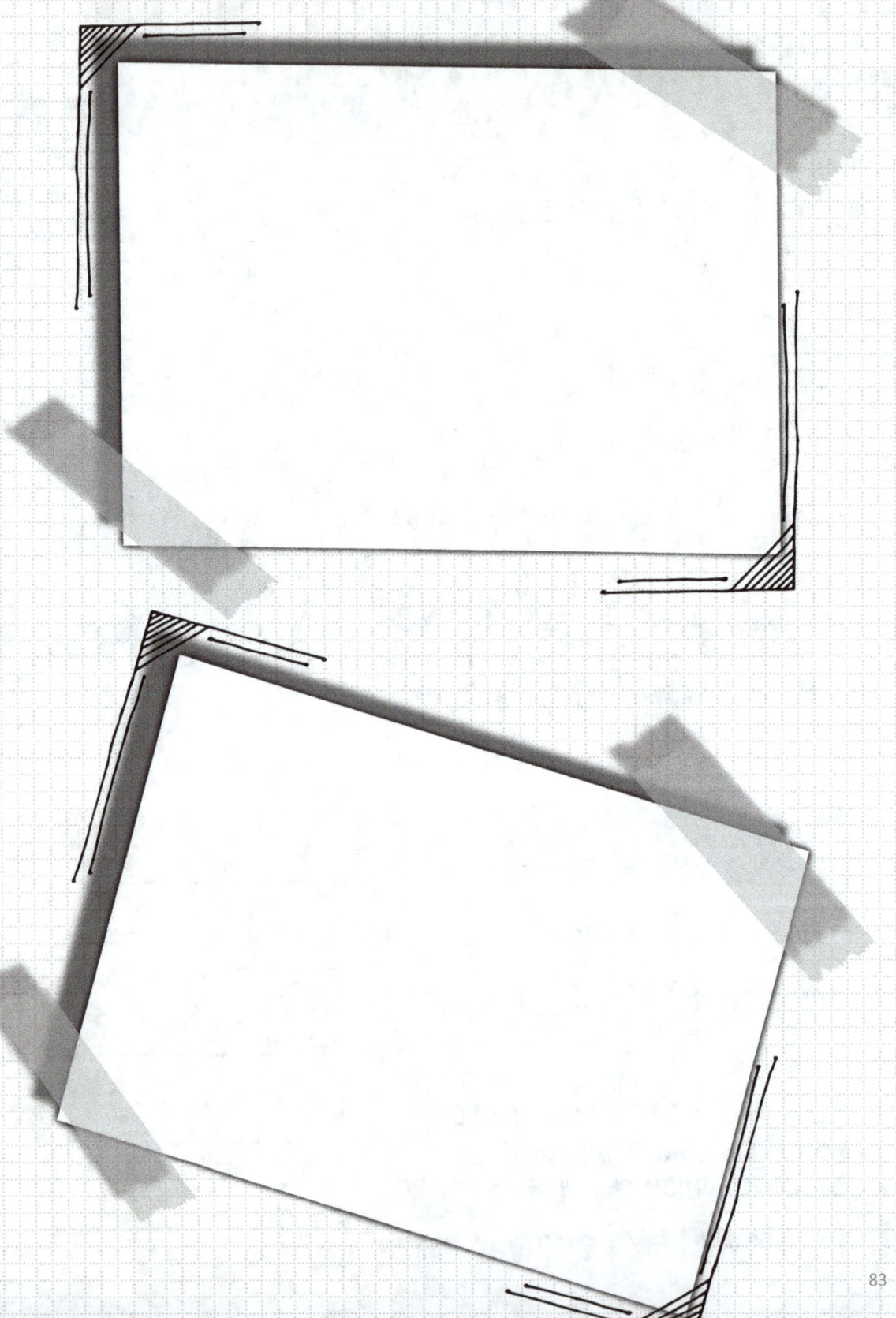

FOCUS : FEEL IT OUT!

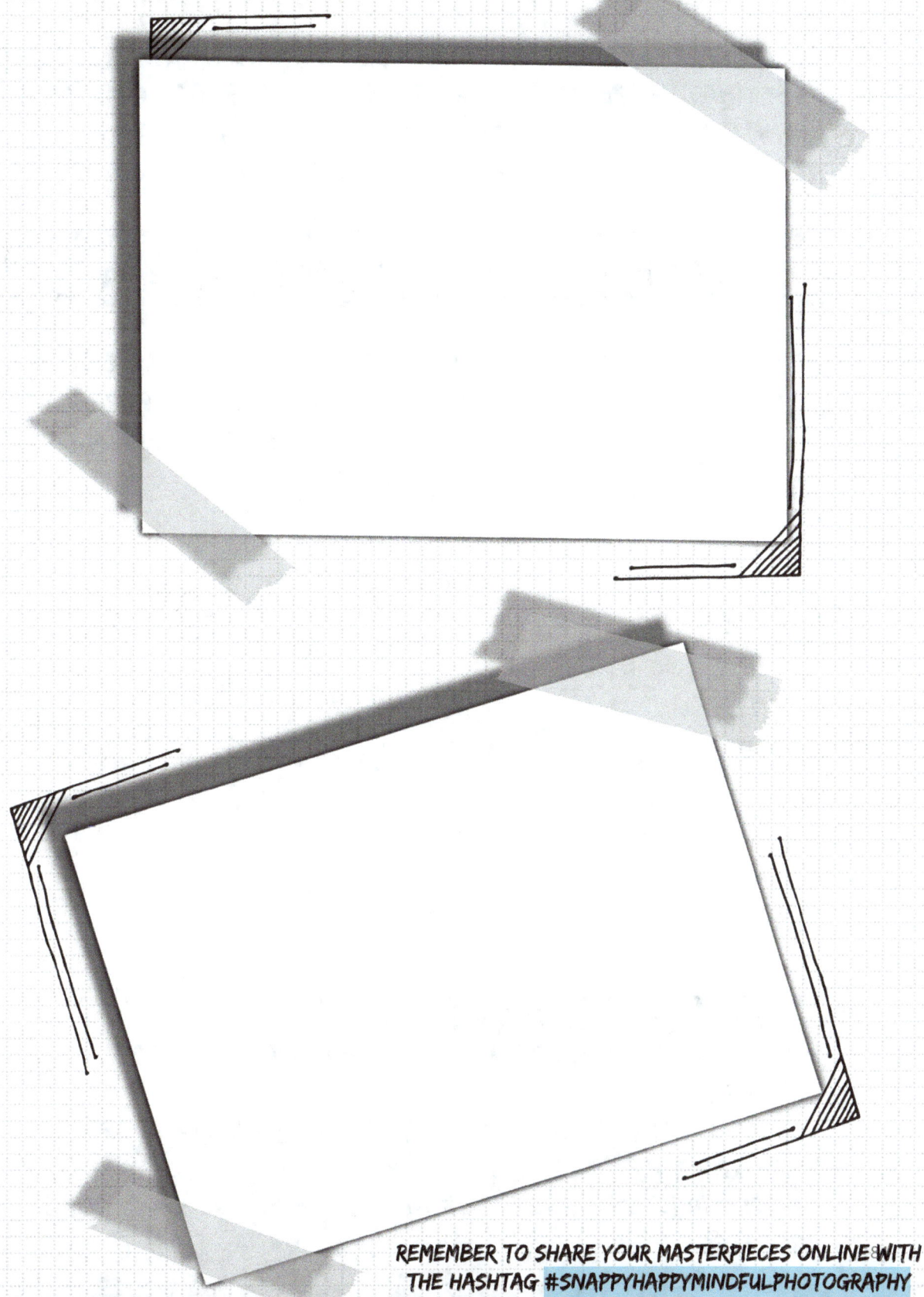

FOCUS : ADIOS, COLOR!

IF COLOR CAN MAKE US FEEL THINGS, BE SYMBOLIC AND CATCH OUR EYE — WHAT HAPPENS WHEN WE TAKE IT OUT? BLACK AND WHITE PHOTOGRAPHS SOMETIMES MAKE PEOPLE FEEL NOSTALGIC, MYSTERIOUS, OR EVEN MAJESTIC!

IT ALSO ALLOWS OUR MIND TO SEE MORE TEXTURES, SHAPES AND LINES INSTEAD OF JUST BRIGHT BURSTS OF COLOR. WOAH, MAGIC!

YOU WILL TAKE ONLY BLACK AND WHITE PHOTOS FOR A WEEK. YOU WILL NOT SWITCH TO COLOR, EVER! EVEN IF IT'S SO TEMPTING. EVEN IF IT'S THE MOST AMAZING FREAKING RAINBOW YOU'VE EVER SEEN IN YOUR LIFE! NOPE.

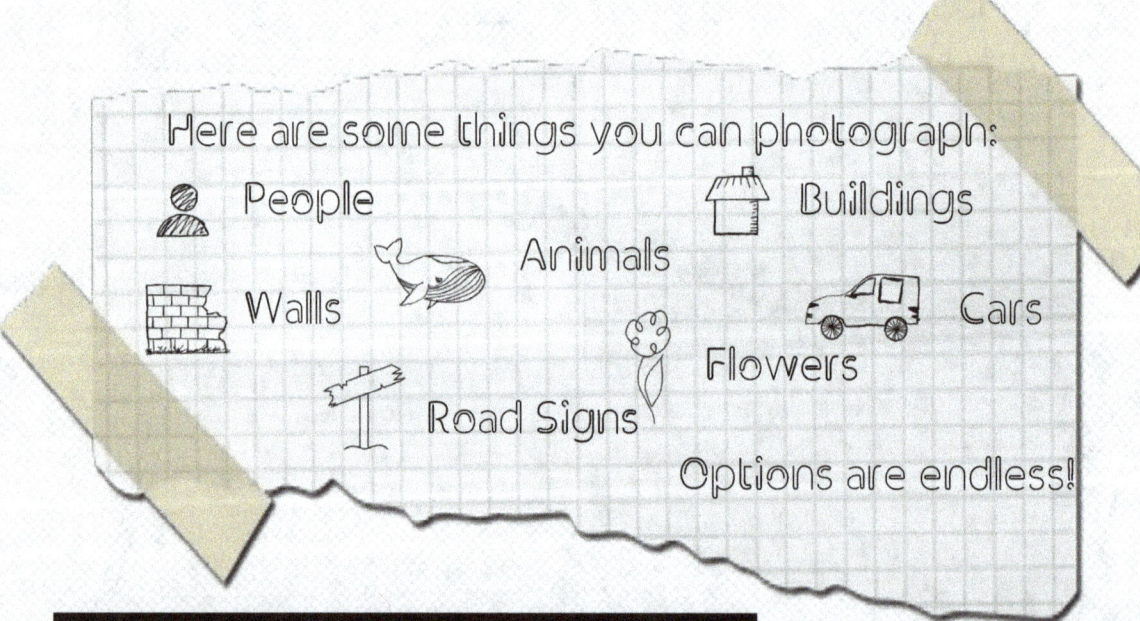

Here are some things you can photograph:

People   Buildings

Animals

Walls   Cars

Flowers

Road Signs

Options are endless!

SOME GOOD QUESTIONS TO ASK YOURSELF:
- ✓ WHAT DOES TAKING PICTURES IN BLACK AND WHITE FEEL LIKE FOR YOU?
- ✓ ARE YOU NOTICING YOURSELF TAKING CERTAIN TYPES OF PICTURES MORE OFTEN?
- ✓ WHEN WOULD YOU USE BLACK AND WHITE PICTURES VS. COLOR PICTURES?

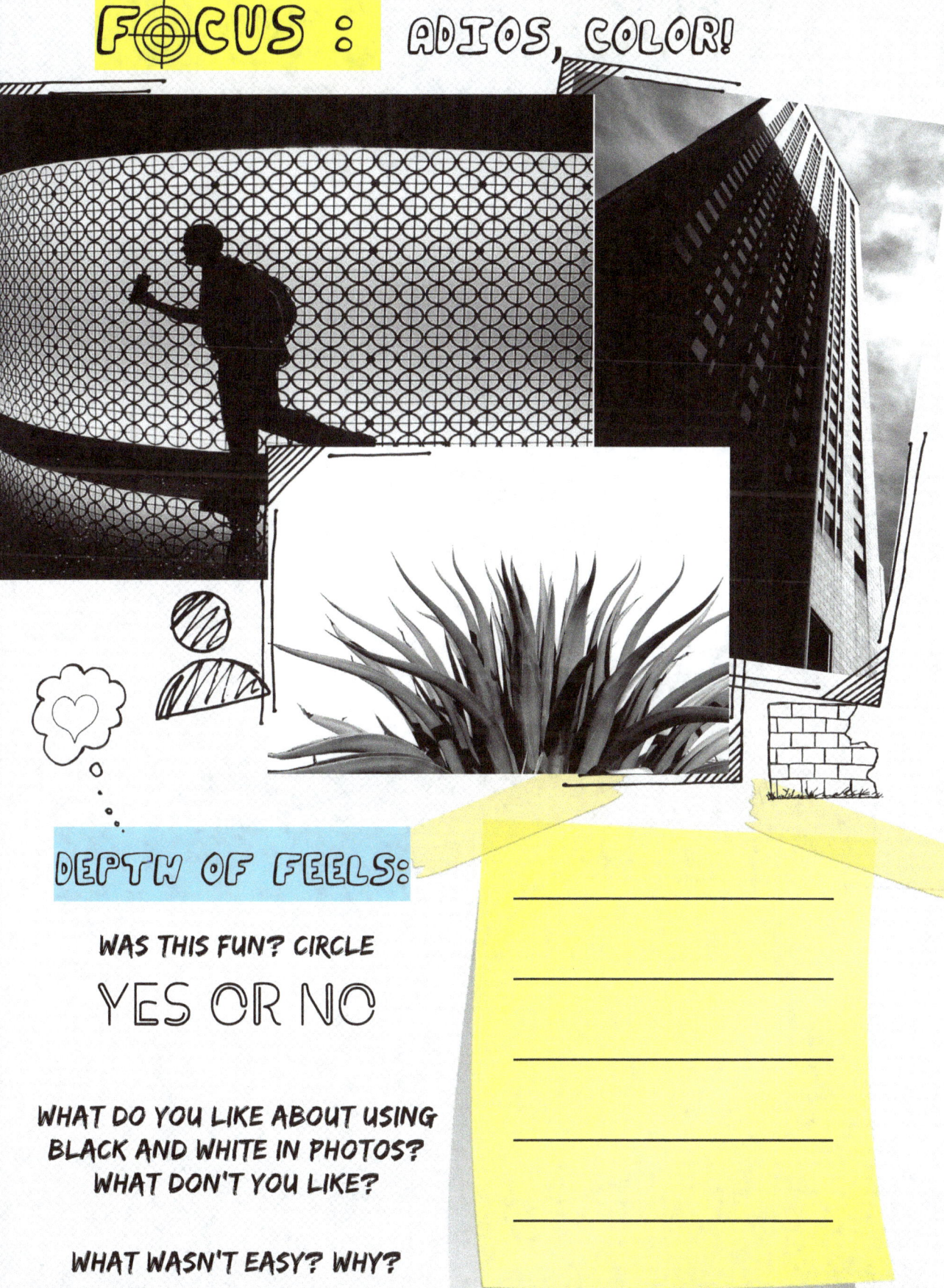

DEPTH OF FEELS:

WAS THIS FUN? CIRCLE

YES OR NO

WHAT DO YOU LIKE ABOUT USING BLACK AND WHITE IN PHOTOS? WHAT DON'T YOU LIKE?

WHAT WASN'T EASY? WHY?

F☉CUS : ADIOS, COLOR!

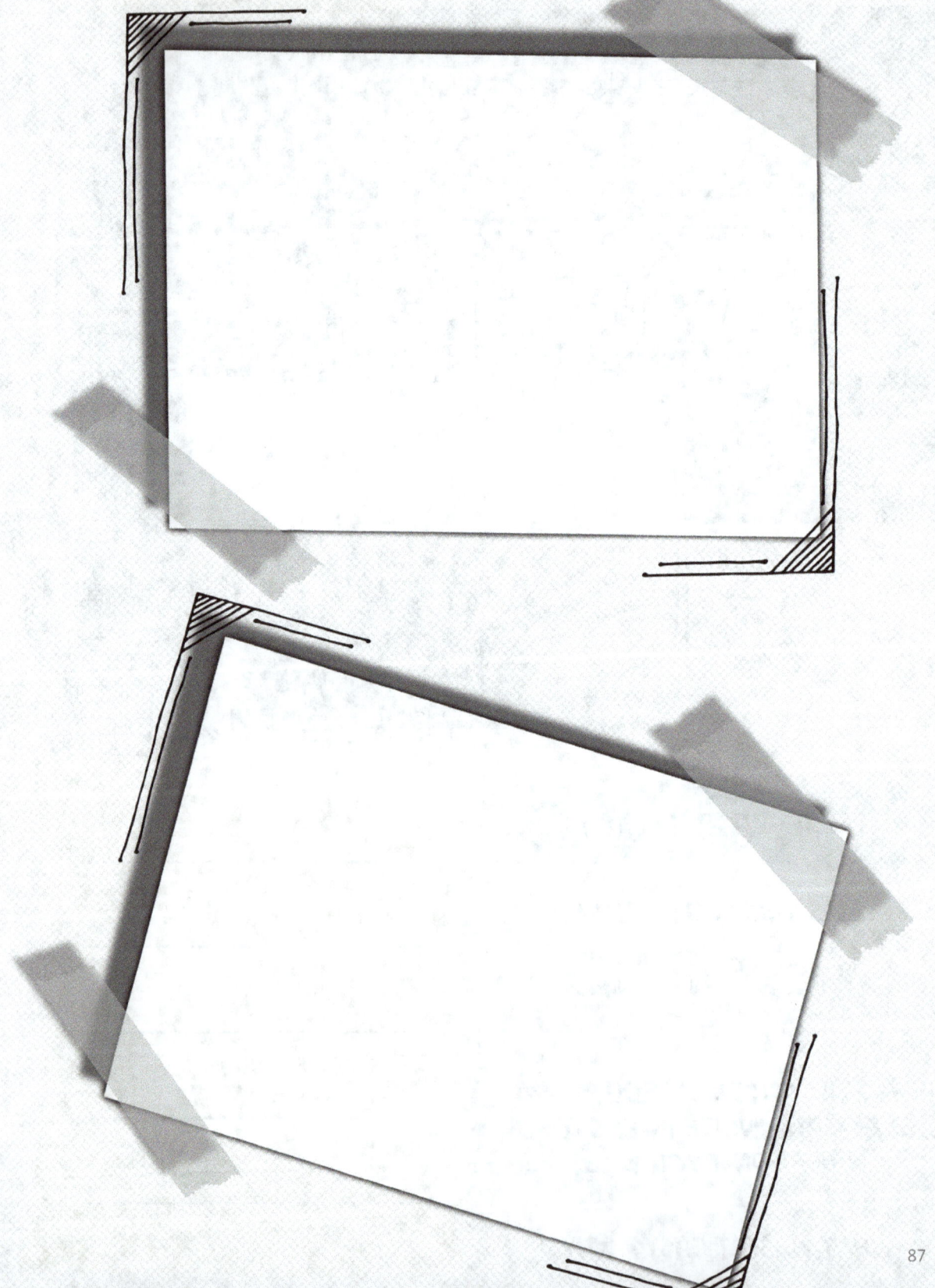

FOCUS : ADIOS COLOR!

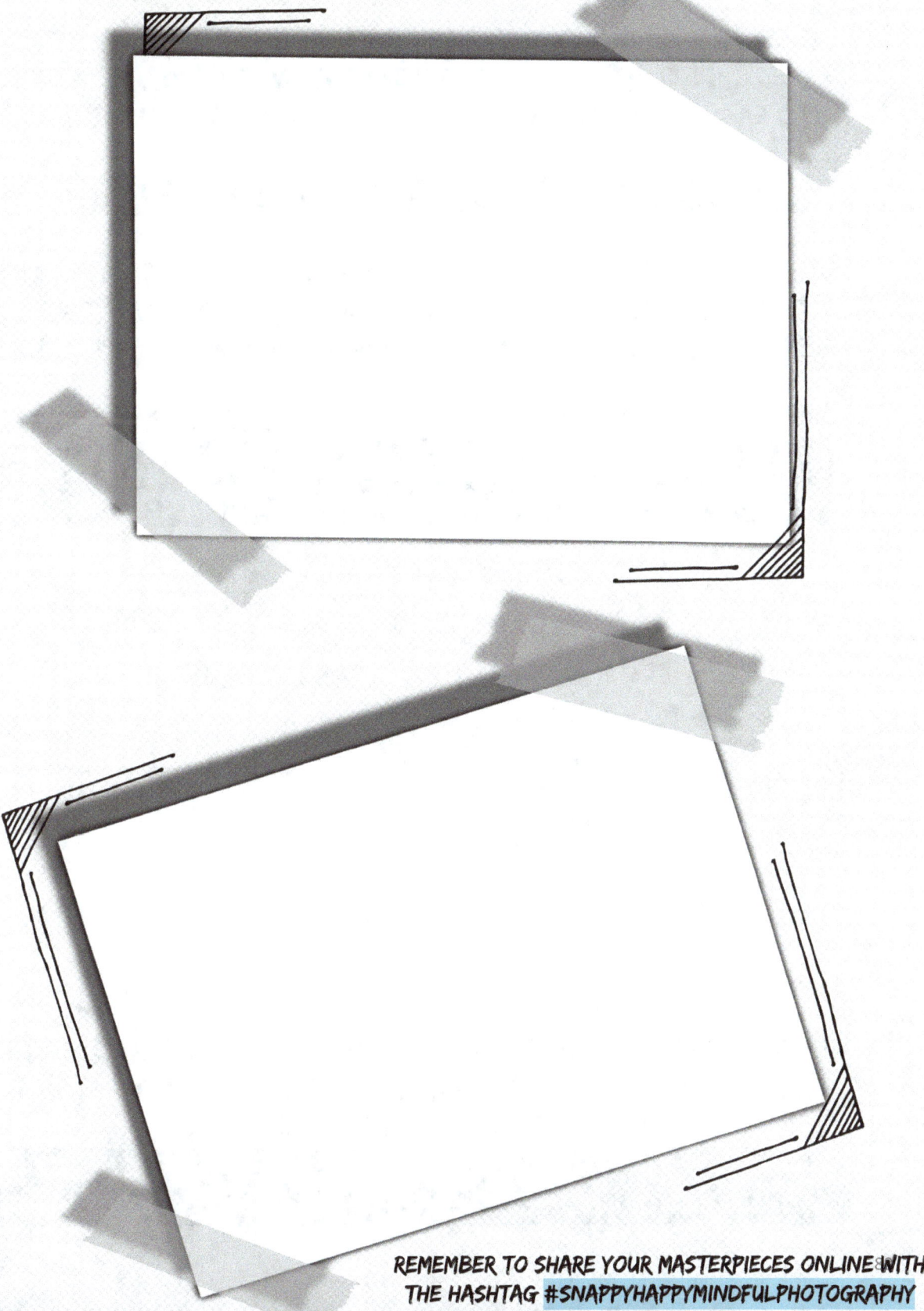

FOCUS : SNAP THE NOT CUTE!

SOMETIMES WE ONLY LOOK FOR SOMETHING THAT IS BEAUTIFUL, PERFECT, IDEAL, OR FLAWLESS TO TAKE A SNAP OF IN THE WORLD. IT'S EASY TO MAKE ALREADY BEAUTIFUL THINGS MORE PRETTY.

BUT WHAT IF WE GO ON A HUNT FOR THE NOT-SO-CUTE?

HAVING THE ATTENTION TOWARDS AND FINDING APPRECIATION IN THE FLAWS OF THE WORLD, IN OURSELVES, AND IN WHAT WE PHOTOGRAPH ALLOWS US TO APPRECIATE THE HONESTY OF IT ALL!

HERE'S WHAT YOU'RE GONNA DO. GO OUT AND FIND SOMETHING THAT'S CRACKING, CHIPPED, FALLING A PART, LOOKS LIKE A HOT MESS, SCREAMS "WHAT IS GOING ON HERE" AND PHOTOGRAPH IT.

Focus on hunting for not cute things:
Rusty buckets, cars or tools
Peeling paint
Shattered glass
Trash on the streets
Cracked driveways

REMEMBER TO USE WHAT YOU KNOW: TEXTURE, BLACK AND WHITE, ANGLES, AND CLOSE-UPS, TO REALLY SEE THE BEAUTY IN WHAT ISN'T NATURALLY CUTE TO LOOK AT.

WHAT DOES IT FEEL LIKE APPRECIATE SOMETHING THAT ISN'T NATURALLY CUTE INTO SOMETHING FLAWLESS LIKE YOUR DREAMS?

FOCUS : SNAP THE NOT CUTE!

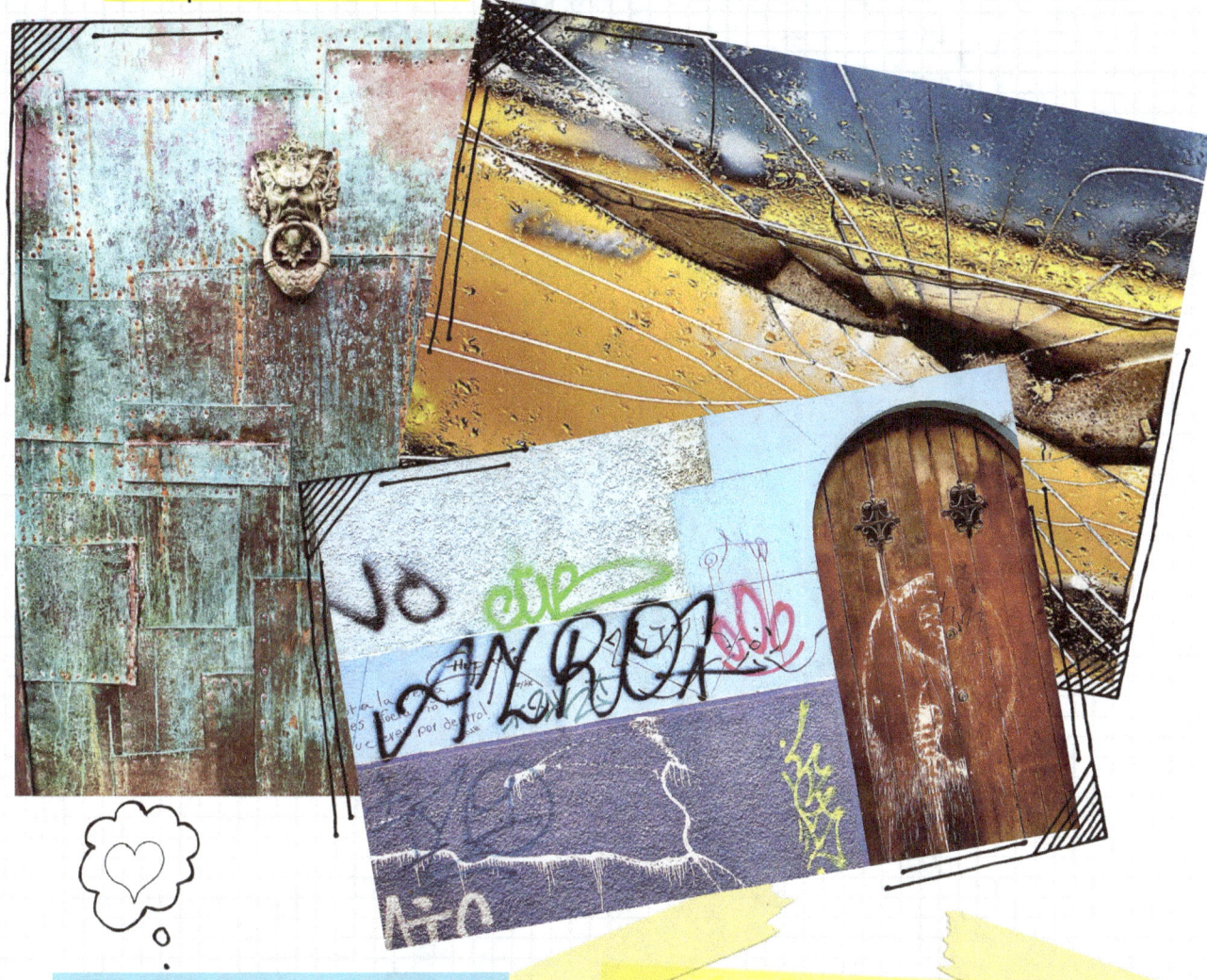

DEPTH OF FEELS:

WAS THIS FUN? CIRCLE

YES OR NO

WHAT DID YOU ENJOY ABOUT MAKING NOT CUTE THINGS MORE PRETTY?

WHAT WASN'T EASY? WHY?

FOCUS : SNAP THE NOT CUTE!

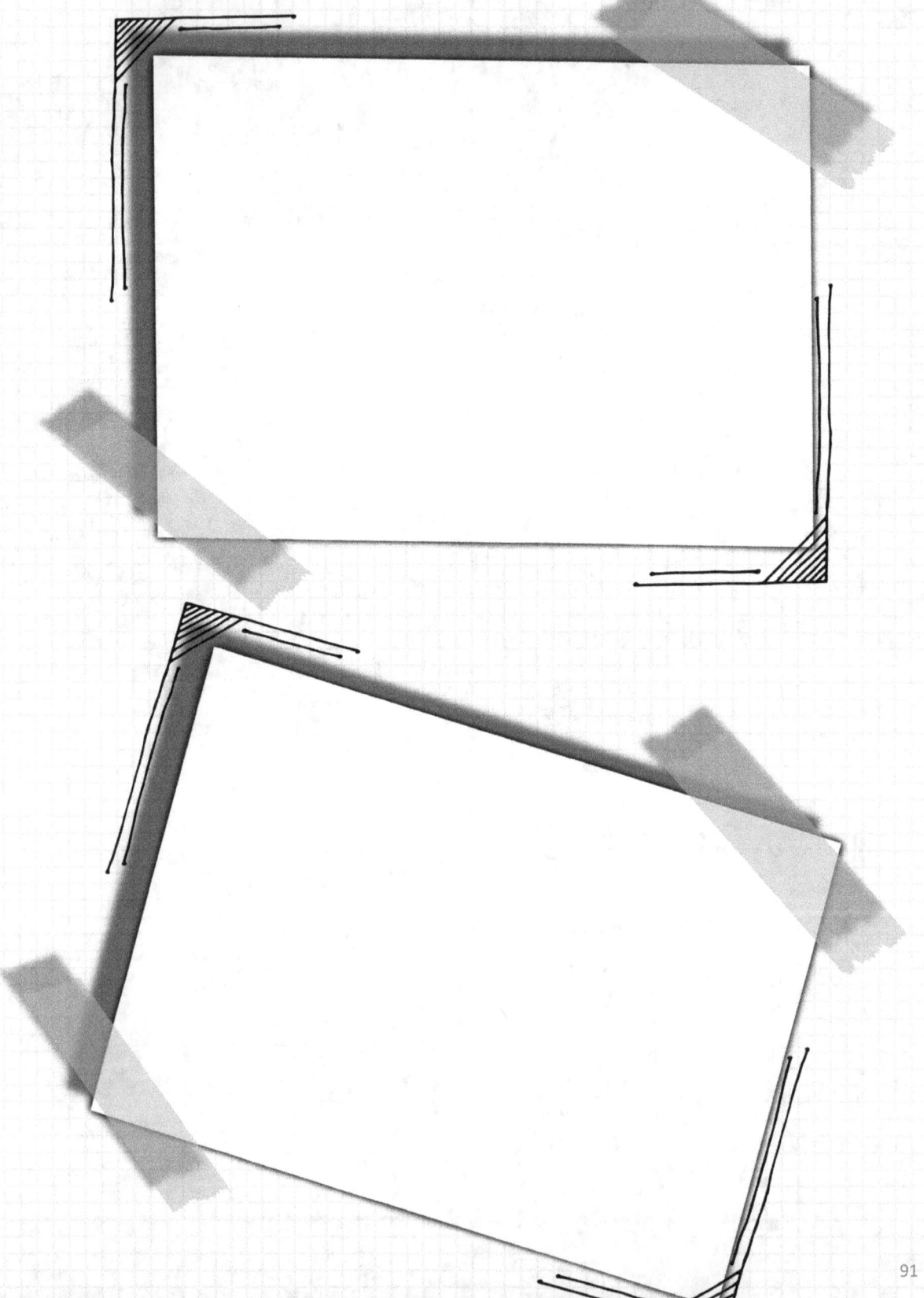

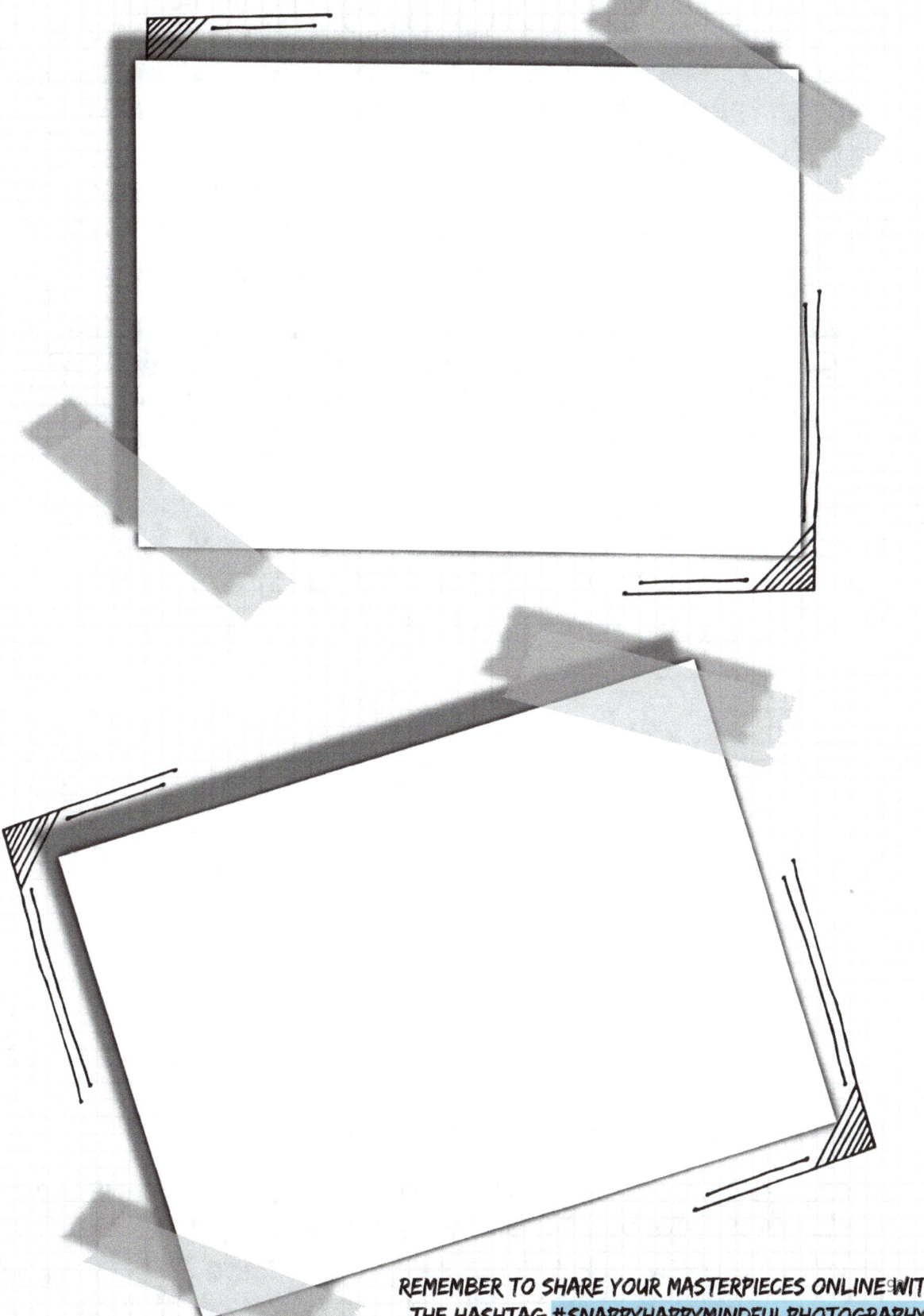

F⊙CUS : NO LOOKING BACK!

GUESS WHAT? ONCE UPON A TIME, YOU COULDN'T IMMEDIATELY SEE YOUR PHOTOGRAPHS. WAAA??? BACK IN THE OLDEN DAYS (AHEM, NOT THAT LONG AGO, I'M BEING EXTRA), YOU USED TO HAVE TO DEVELOP YOUR PICTURES WHICH DEPENDING ON MANY THINGS, COULD TAKE A LONG TIME — THAT MEANT YOU HAD NO IDEA IF YOUR PHOTOS TURNED OUT! AND IT WAS KINDA COOL BECAUSE IT WAS A SURPRISE IF YOU FORGOT WHAT YOU PHOTOGRAPHED.

LIFE IS KINDA LIKE THAT, TOO, RIGHT? SOMETIMES WE CAN'T CHANGE WHAT WE DID, BUT ONLY LEARN AND TRY SOMETHING DIFFERENT IF THE OUTCOME ISN'T WHAT WE EXPECTED.

TRY THIS: DON'T LOOK AT THE PHOTOS YOU TAKE. NOT EVEN A PEAK. JUST SNAP A PIC, AND MOVE ON. TAKE AS MANY PICS AS YOU WANT, BUT DON'T LOOK. DON'T CHEAT, AND TRY TO CHECK IF IT TURNED OUT.

How it works:

1.) Snap a photo, anything you like.

2) Don't look at the photo at all.

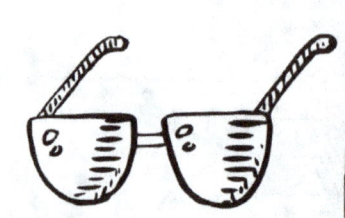

3.) Snap more photos, as many as you want.

4.) One week later visit the photos you took.

5.) Having time away from the pics, how does it feel?

FUN TIP:

IF YOU HAVE ACCESS, TRY USING AN OLD-SCHOOL 35MM CAMERA WITH FILM OR A DISPOSABLE CAMERA. THEN WAIT TO GET THE PHOTOS DEVELOPED. THEN YOU'LL REALLY GET THE FEELING OF NOT HAVING CONTROL OF WHAT YOU SEE AND HOW YOU SEE IT!

FOCUS : NO LOOKING BACK!

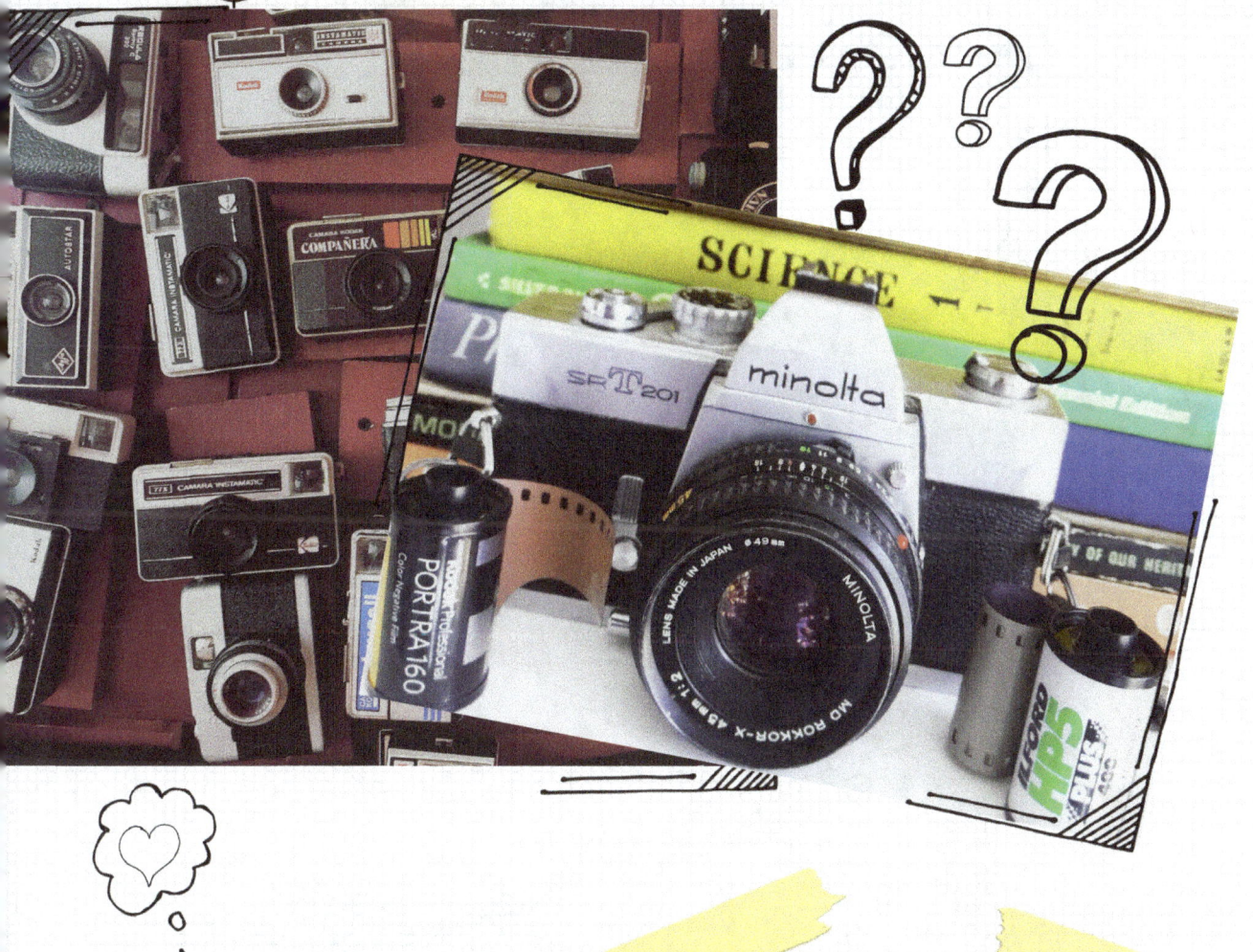

DEPTH OF FEELS:

WAS THIS FUN? CIRCLE

YES OR NO

WHAT DOES IT FEEL LIKE TO HAVE TO WAIT TO SEE YOUR PHOTOS? WHAT DOES THAT TIME DO FOR YOU?

WHAT WASN'T EASY? WHY?

_____

_____

_____

_____

_____

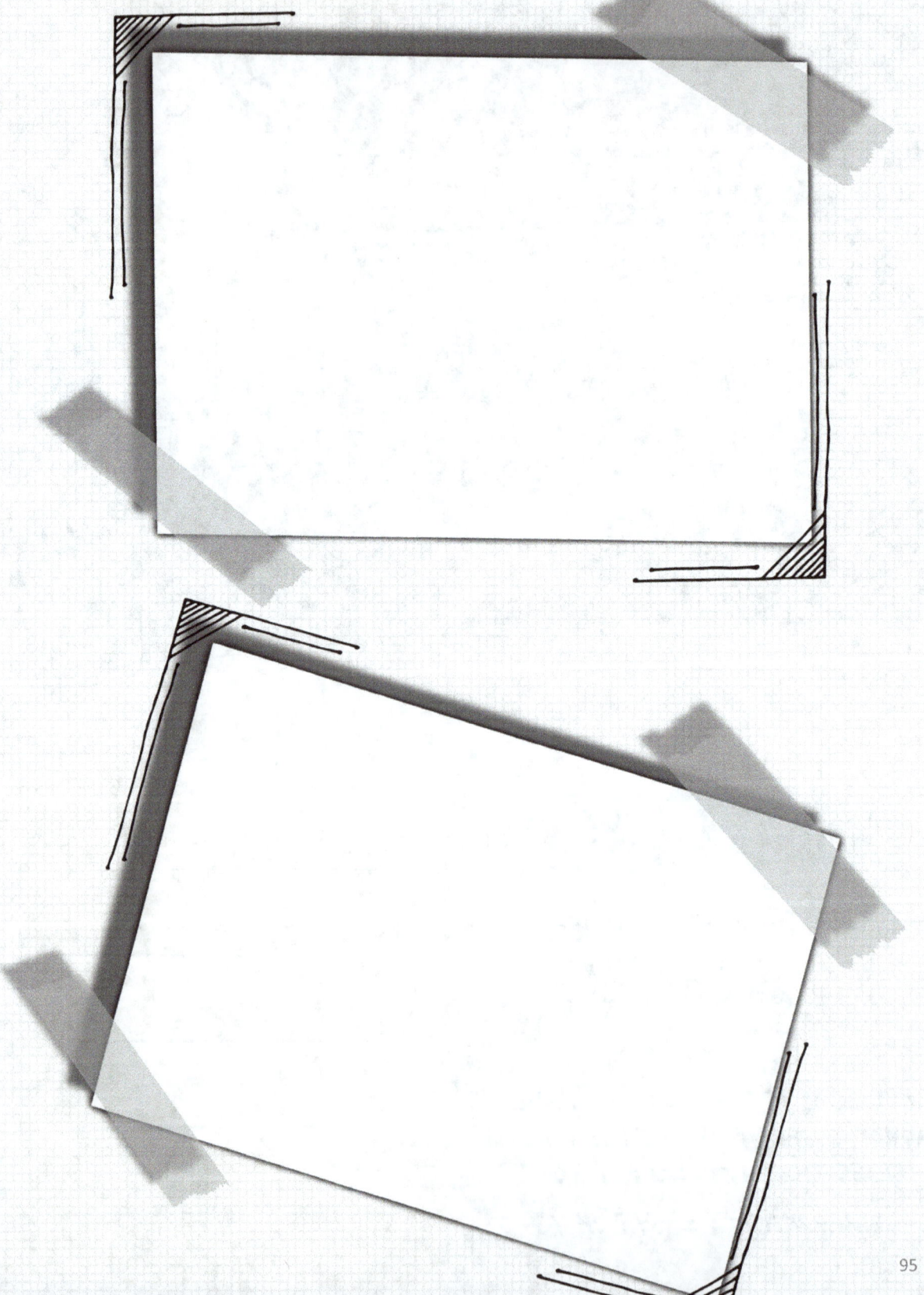

FOCUS : NO LOOKING BACK!

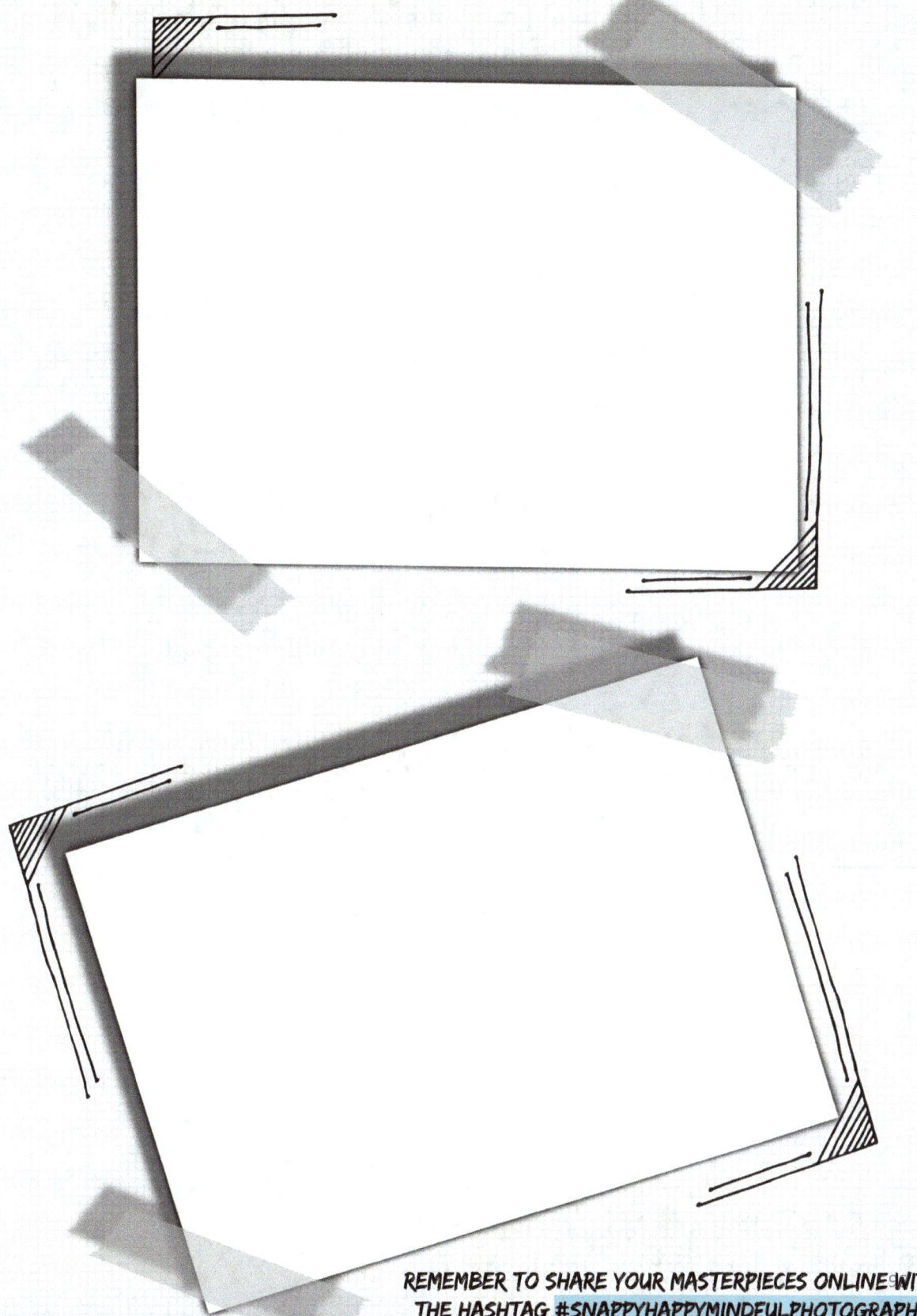

"THE CAMERA IS

AN INSTRUMENT

THAT TEACHES

PEOPLE TO SEE

WITHOUT A

CAMERA." — DORTHEA LANGE

THINK ABOUT IT

USE THIS PAGE IN ANY WAY YOU'D LIKE, BUT CAN WE MAKE A SUGGESTION? MAYBE WRITE DOWN SOME NOTES ABOUT HOW YOU ARE FEELING AND LEARNING SOME OF THESE WAYS TO EXPLORE WITH THE CAMERA. ARE YOU HAVING FUN? WHY OR WHY NOT? ARE YOU FEELING DIFFERENT THAN WHEN YOU STARTED BEFORE THIS BOOK? HOW SO? OR YOU CAN DRAW A PICTURE, OR YOU CAN SHARE SOME PHOTOS. YOU DO YOU, BOO!

F⊕CUS : RELAX THE ROUTINE!

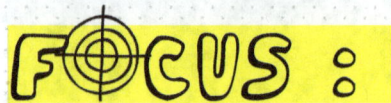

IT'S EASY TO GET STUCK IN HABITS AND PATTERNS WITHOUT EVEN THINKING THEY ARE CAUSING US TO MISS OUT ON NEW OR DIFFERENT EXPERIENCES!

ROUTINES CAN BE GOOD, TOTALLY! THEY ALSO CAN CAUSE US TO GLIDE THROUGH OUR DAY NOT NOTICING. THAT AIN'T GOOD.

YOU WILL FOCUS ON BREAKING YOUR HABIT OF DOING THE SAME THING EVERY DAY BY PHOTOGRAPHING TWO THINGS: SUNSETS AND SUNRISES. MAYBE YOU HATE GETTING UP EARLY... GUESS WHAT? TIME TO CHANGE THAT ROUTINE! MAYBE YOU DON'T STAY UP LATE ENOUGH FOR A SUNSET... BOOP! NOW YOU WILL! MAYBE YOU ARE NEVER OUTSIDE TO SEE THEM. HERE. WE. GO!

Here's how to photograph sunsets/sunrises:

! Find out what time the sun rises/sets and set an Alarm for a 1/2 hour before. Snap away!

Fun fact: The light that glows 1/2 before sunset and after sunrise is called "The GOLDEN HOUR"

Psst: some of the best pictures can be taken during the Golden Hour(!)

SOME HELPFUL TIPS:

✓ PHOTOGRAPH SUNRISE/SETS ON DIFFERENT DAYS. SEE WHAT CHANGES, COLORS, AND MORE.
✓ FEEL YOUR BODY WHEN YOU CHANGE YOUR ROUTINE: ARE YOU SLEEPY BECAUSE YOU'RE UP EARLIER? HOW DOES IT FEEL?
✓ NOTICE WHAT OTHER THINGS YOU NOTICE NOW THAT YOU ARE SWITCHING YOUR ROUTINE. HOW DOES THAT FEEL?

FOCUS : RELAX THE ROUTINE!

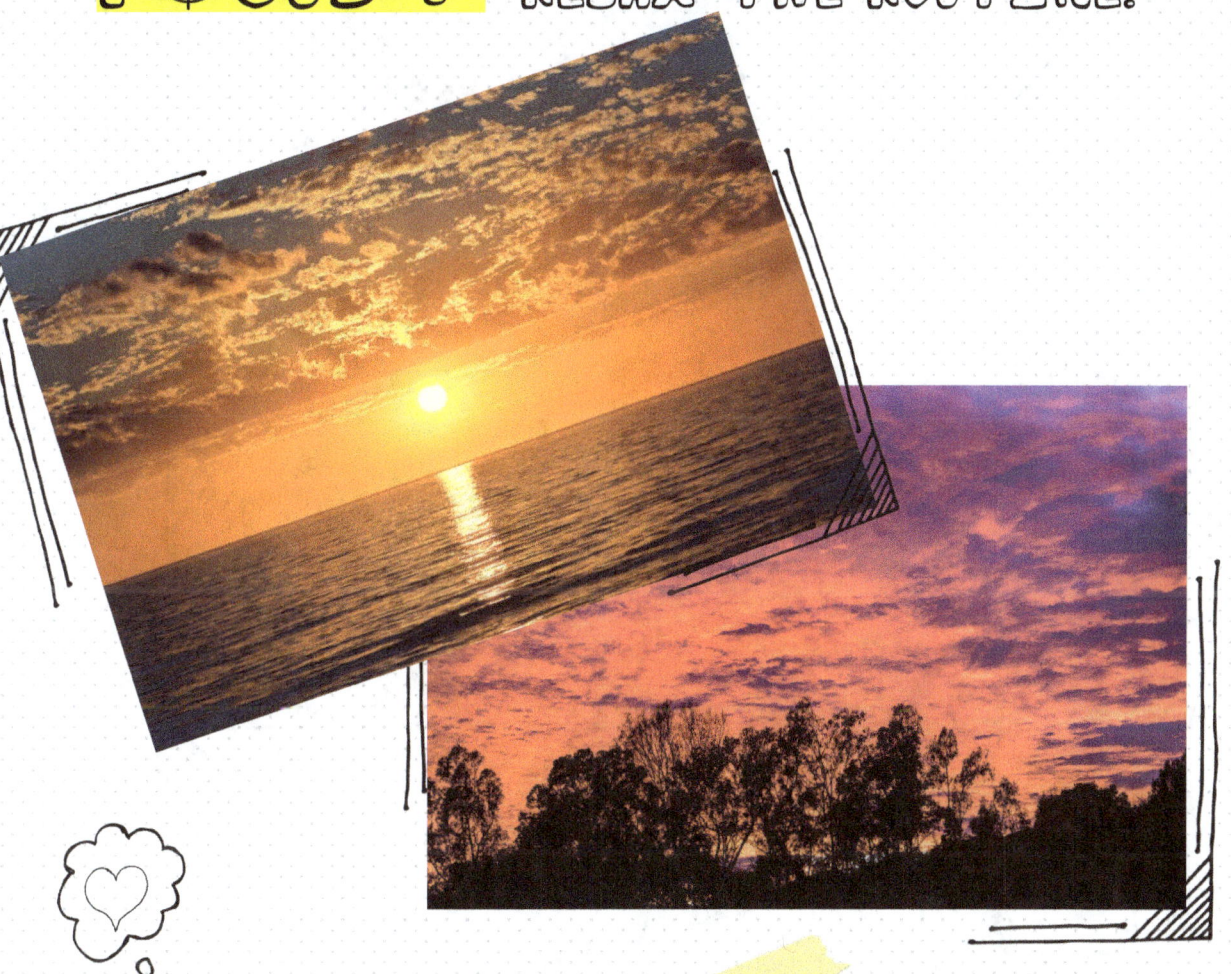

DEPTH OF FEELS:

WAS THIS FUN? CIRCLE

YES OR NO

HOW DID IT FEEL TO CHANGE YOUR
ROUTINE? WILL YOU MAKE NEW
ROUTINES NOW?

WHAT WASN'T EASY? WHY?

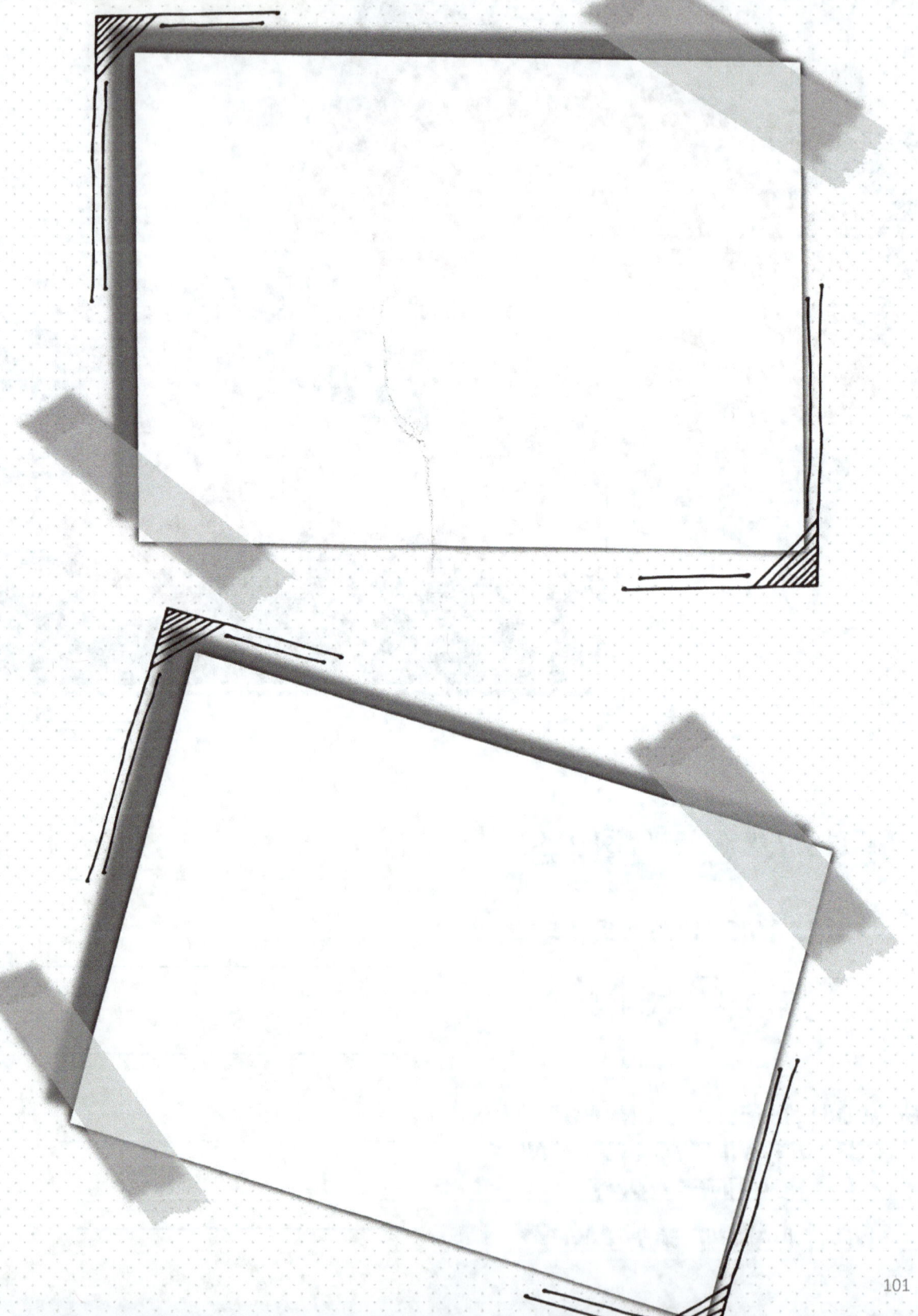

101

F⊙CUS : RELAX THE ROUTINE!

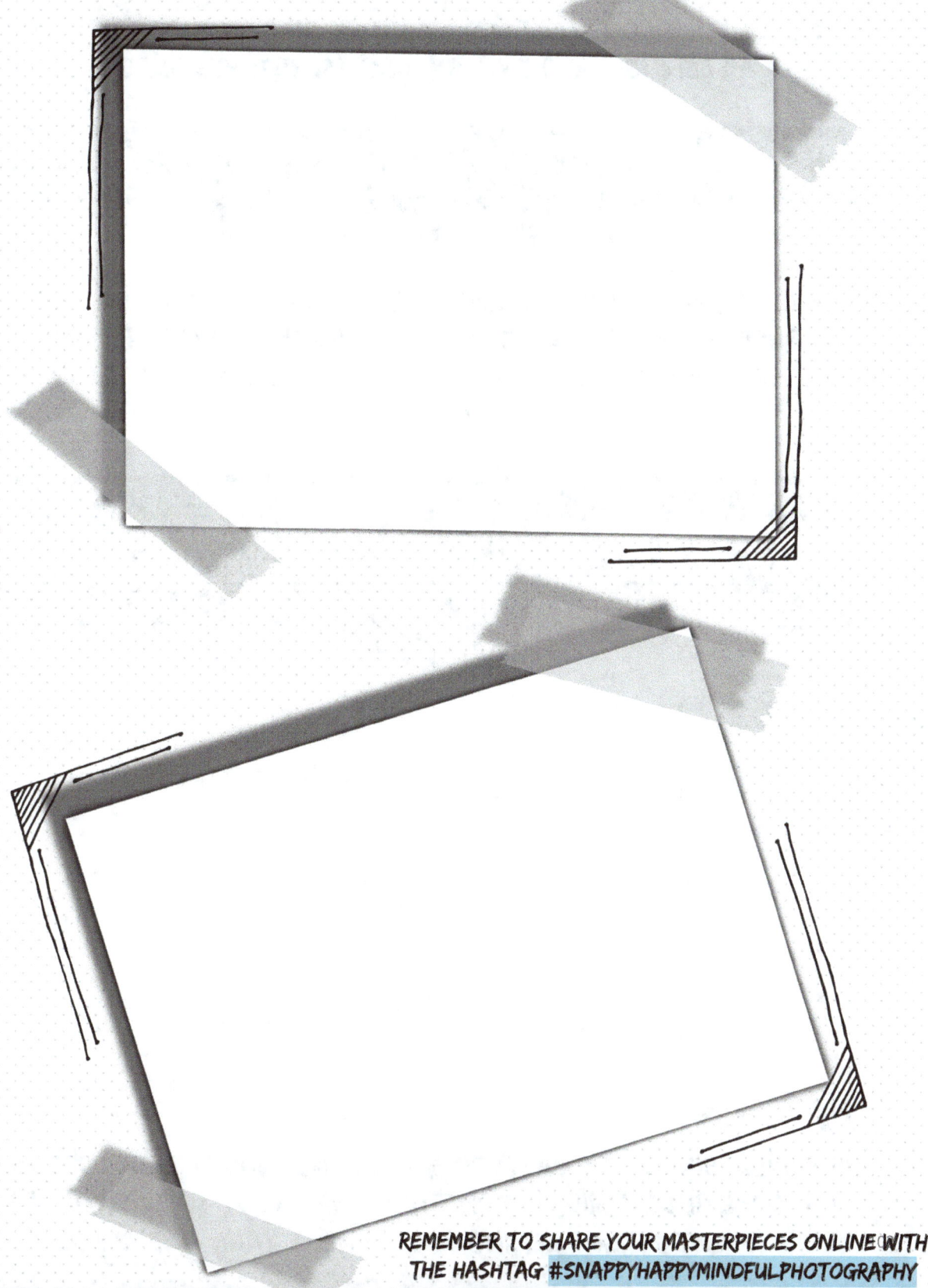

F⊙CUS : SNAP ALL THE SENSES!

WAIT, HUH? HOW DO YOU TAKE A PICTURE OF A SOUND... A TASTE... A FEELING, OR EVEN A SMELL? *SCRATCHES HEAD*

WE USE OUR EYES SO OFTEN IN PHOTOGRAPHY THAT WE OFTEN FORGET THAT OTHER SENSES THAT ARE PART OF OURSELVES SHOULD BE EXPRESSED IN ART IN SOME WAY.

DOCUMENTING A SENSE IS KINDA TRICKY, BUT HOW COULD YOU DO THAT USING IMAGES AND EMOTIONS THROUGH A CAMERA? MAYBE A CLOSE-UP OF GRASS FOR THE SMELL OF A FRESHLY CUT LAWN? MAYBE

THESE COULD BE ABSTRACT PHOTOS, OR YOU COULD LITERALLY DOCUMENT THE ITEM THAT GIVES THE SENSE. BUT WITH THIS ADVENTURE, WHILE SNAPPING, THINK ABOUT THE SENSES YOU USE EVERY SINGLE DAY TO EXPLORE THIS WORLD AND CELEBRATE THEM IN A PHOTO!

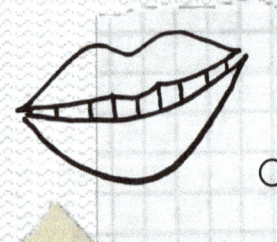

Here's a list of all the senses to snap!

- o SIGHT
- o SMELLING
- o HEARING
- o TASTING
- o SEEING

FUN TIP:

DON'T OVERTHINK IF IT'S CAPTURING THE SENSE JUST RIGHT. LIKE ABSTRA
ART, SOMETIMES IT MEANS SOMETHING DIFFERENT TO EVERYONE! SOME
PHOTOS MIGHT REMIND YOU OF MORE THAN ONE SENSE!

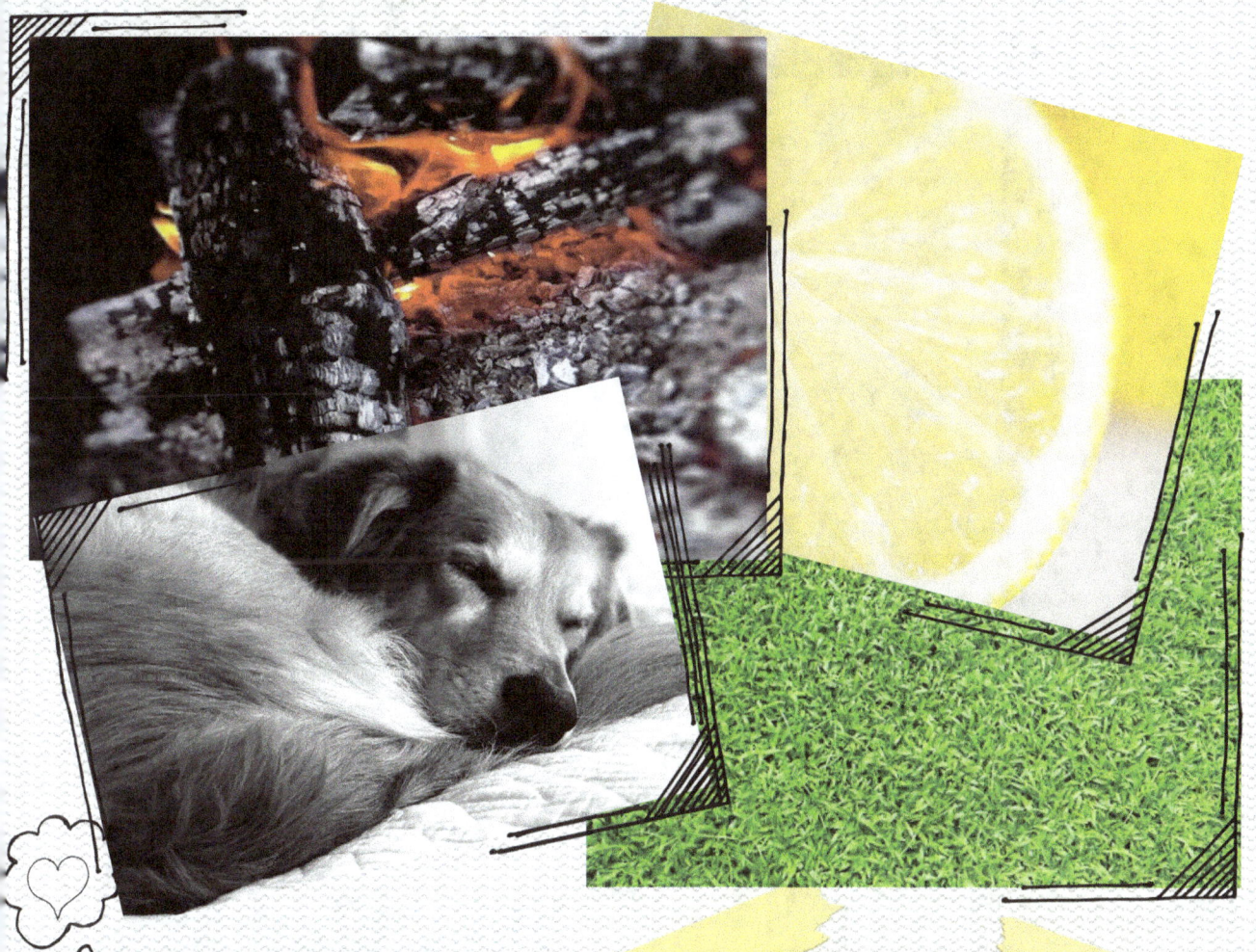

DEPTH OF FEELS:

WWAS THIS FUN? CIRCLE

YES OR NO

DID YOU FIND THAT SOME PHOTOS
YOU TOOK DOCUMENTED MORE THAN
ONE SENSE? WHY IS THAT?

WHAT WASN'T EASY? WHY?

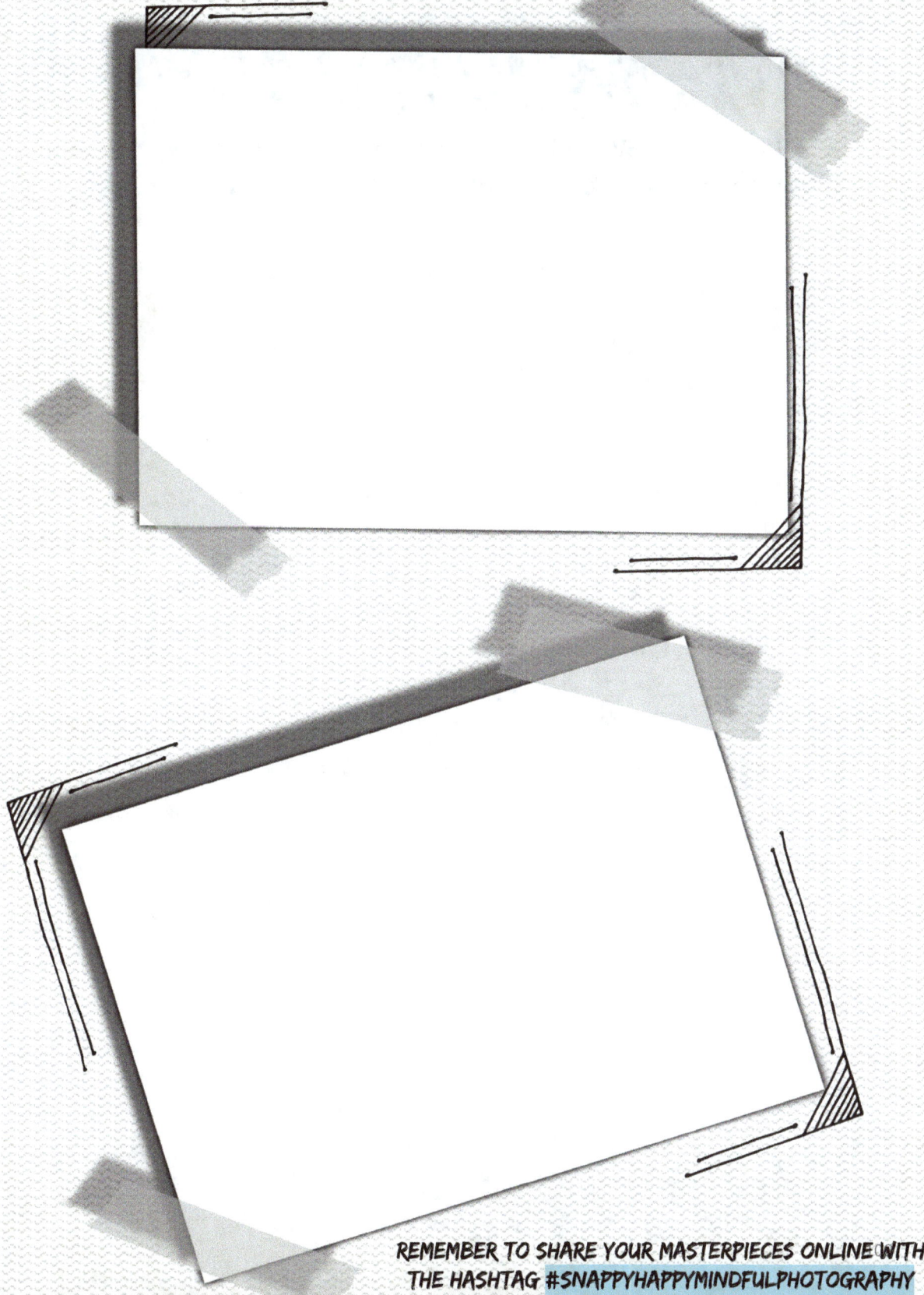

THINK ABOUT IT

YOU'VE COME TO THE END OF THIS JOURNEY AND HAVE HAD MANY EXPLORATIONS. WHICH ACTIVITY WAS YOUR FAVORITE? WHY? WHICH ACTIVITY ARE YOU GOING TO KEEP DOING?

WHICH ACTIVITY WAS THE MOST CHALLENGING? WHY? WOULD YOU CHANGE ANYTHING ABOUT YOUR EXPERIENCE?

GLOSSARY

PHOTOGRAPHY TERMS

THESE ARE THE MORE SIMPLISTIC DEFINITIONS OF THESE TERMS JUST TO GET YOU STARTED! IF YOU'RE INTERESTED IN MORE TECHNICAL PHOTOGRAPHY TERMS, THERE ARE PLENTY OF RESOURCES TO FILL YOUR BRAIN!

DEPTH OF FIELD

THE DISTANCE BETWEEN THE NEAREST AND THE FURTHEST OBJECTS THAT GIVE AN IMAGE JUDGED TO BE IN FOCUS IN A CAMERA.

EXPOSURE

THE AMOUNT OF LIGHT THAT ENTERS YOUR CAMERA TO MAKE THE PICTURE.

TOO MUCH LIGHT: TOO BRIGHT
NOT ENOUGH: TOO DARK

FOCUS

THE SHARP PART OF AN IMAGE

LENS

THE CURVE THAT LIGHT COMES IN TO AND HELPS CREATE THE PICTURE WITH SOME HELP INSIDE OF YOUR CAMERA.

IT'S HOW YOUR CAMERA SEES THE WORLD!

SHUTTER

THE DEVICE IN THE CAMERA THAT LETS LIGHT IN. THINK OF IT AS A BLINKING EYE

MINDFUL TERMS

THERE'S A LOT MORE DEFINITION TO THESE TERMS, TOO. BUT DOESN'T HURT TO JUMP IN AND LEARN SOMEWHERE!

Non-Judgmental

LET GO OF HAVING AN OPINION ABOUT SOMETHING OR SOMEONE. JUST NOTICE IT AND DON'T TRY TO THINK OF WHETHER IT'S GOOD, BAD, OR OK TO YOU.

Observation

JUST NOTICE WHAT IS HAPPENING OR WHAT YOU ARE SEEING RIGHT NOW. USE YOUR SENSES: SIGHT, SMELL, HEAR, TASTE, AND TOUCH

Trust

BELIEVE YOUR PRACTICE WILL HELP YOU GROW WITHOUT FEAR

Curiosity

ASK QUESTIONS ABOUT WHAT IS WORKING AND WHAT ISN'T WORKING. REFLECT AND SEE WHAT YOU CAN LEARN. ASK YOURSELF:
WHAT IS WORKING?
WHAT AM I FEELING?
WHY AM I FEELING LIKE THIS?

Presence

BE HERE. RIGHT NOW. YOUR BRAIN IS NOWHERE ELSE BUT RIGHT WHERE YOU ARE NOW

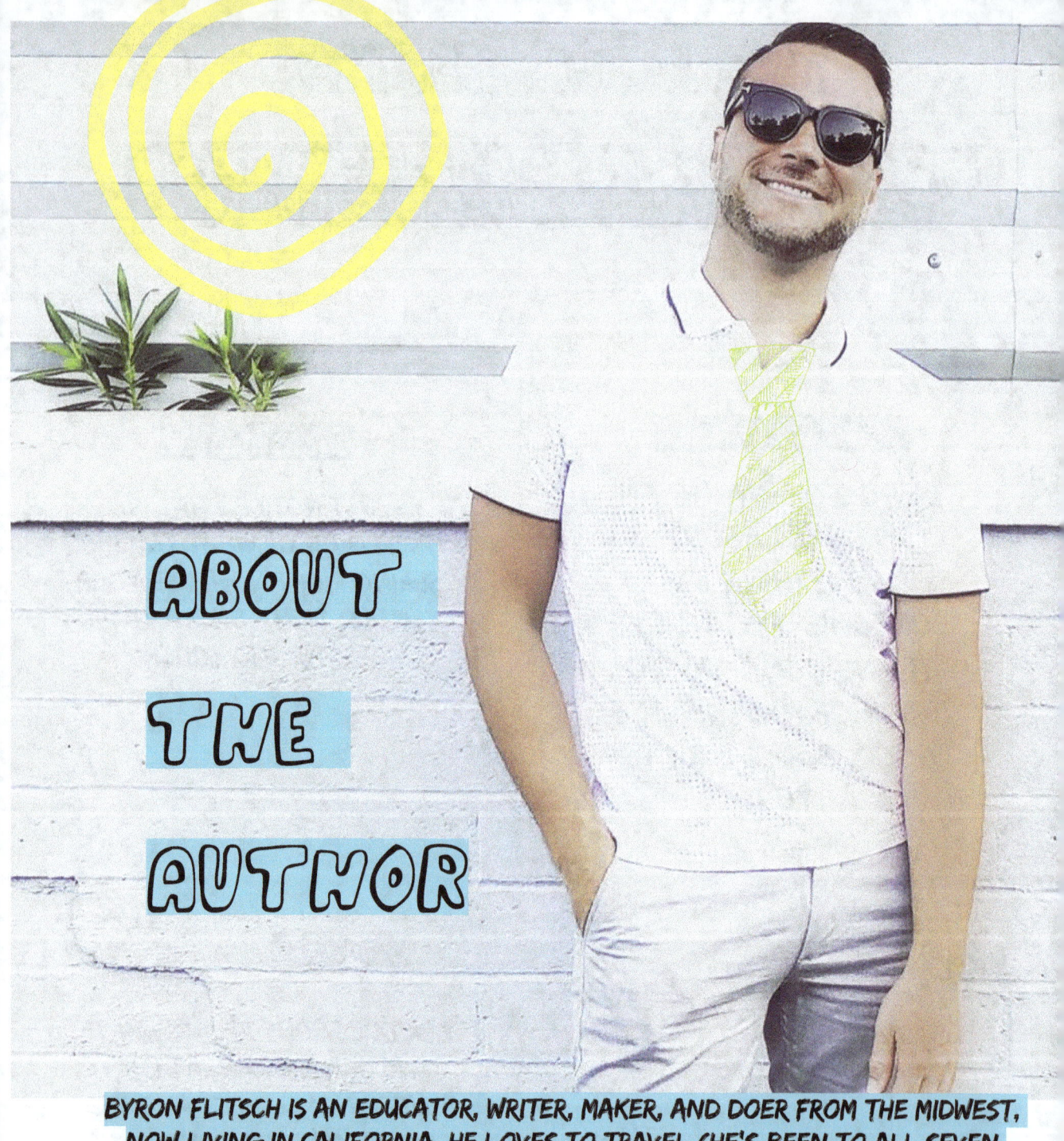

ABOUT THE AUTHOR

BYRON FLITSCH IS AN EDUCATOR, WRITER, MAKER, AND DOER FROM THE MIDWEST, NOW LIVING IN CALIFORNIA. HE LOVES TO TRAVEL (HE'S BEEN TO ALL SEVEN CONTINENTS!), TAKE FUN PICTURES (HE'S BEEN DOING IT SINCE HE WAS 8!), AND NAPPING WITH HIS DOGS (THEY ARE THE BEST CUDDLERS!).

BYRON HAS WORKED WITH MANY INCREDIBLE PEOPLE AND FOUND WHO HAVE HELPED HIM ON HIS MINDFUL JOURNEY. HE'S CERTIFIED IN MINDFUL EDUCATION FOR CHILDREN, CREDENTIALED IN PHOTOGRAPHY EDUCATION AND LIFE COACHING, AND REALLY LIKES PUTTING ALL THREE TOGETHER. HE ALSO RUNS *YOU ARE HERE*, A PLACE FOR GRATITUDE. VISIT HIS WEBSITE: WWW.BYRONFLITSCH.COM

IT'S STORY TIME!

Once upon a time, a young man (spoiler alert: me!) went to a beautiful art school in a far-off kingdom called Chicago, Illinois, to become a photographer. He loved learning, working with different teachers, and hanging with cool new friends that liked making art, too.

But one thing was always missing for our dear young guy (hi, me again!). It always felt like the perfect picture was the goal and not also the process of taking the picture.

Did photography really have to be about the best light, best frame, best subject, and best angle? What about the feeling of photography and the process of making pictures? Could it be a tool to explore and document who we are on the inside as much as it helps us explore and document what we see on the outside? All the questions!?

That's when he started exploring the magical world of mindful photography and created this book for you. And he lived happily ever after.

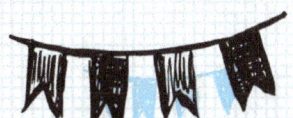 THE END.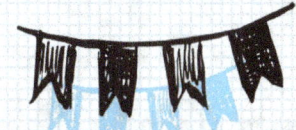

ACKNOWLEDGMENTS!

I WANT TO THANK MY PARENTS FOR CHEERING ME ON THROUGH PHOTO SCHOOL (AND, AHEM, FOOTING SOME OF THE BILLS!). UNWAVERING GRATITUDE TO MY PARTNER, NATE, FOR ROOTING ME IN ALL MY ENDEAVORS. TO MY BROTHER FOR KNOWING HOW TO KEEP ME GROUNDED. MY FRIENDS, JOSH EISENBERG AND MOLLY EACH SUPPORTED MY IDEAS AND HELPED ME EDIT THIS PUPPY.

A VERY SPECIAL SHOUT OUT TO THE MANY MINDFULNESS COACHES SUPPORTING MY JOURNEY. LISL BONDSMITH, MINDFUL SCHOOLS, ABBY WILLS, LAURIE COUSINS, ANJALI DEVA, LIV SILVESTRI, GENEVIEVE RICKON, ANNA ADSIT, AND MY FELLOW AVESON RETREAT CREW FOR THE MINDFUL MEMORIES.

BIG GRATITUDE FOR ALEX MURAVEV'S CLIPART (VIA NOUN PROJECT). YOUR ART MADE THIS BOOK POP!

TO ARTISTS AND PHOTOGRAPHERS THAT BRAVELY CREATE FOR US ALL TO ENJOY. TO YOU, LITTLE SNAP HAPPY FRIENDS. YOU ARE GOING TO CHANGE THE WORLD.

AND BEYONCÉ. YOU SHOULD ALWAYS THANK BEYONCÉ.

VISIT US ONLINE!

GALLERY!　　**EDUCATOR IDEAS!**

MORE ACTIVITIES!　　**ONLINE CLASSES!**

STORE!

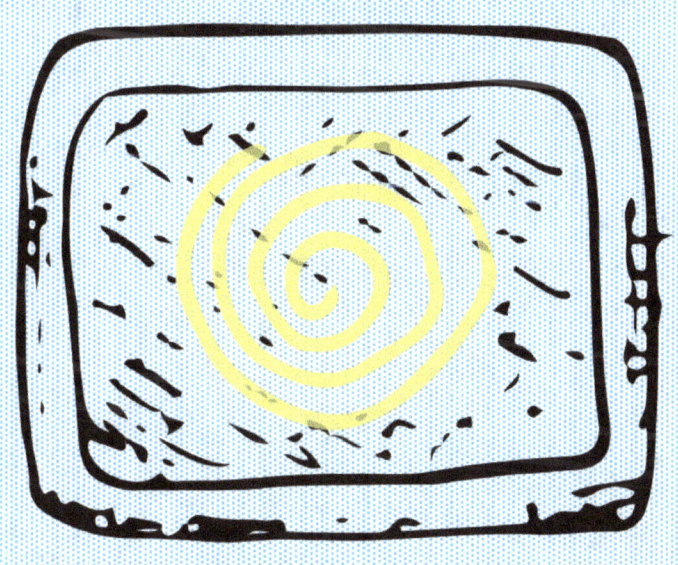

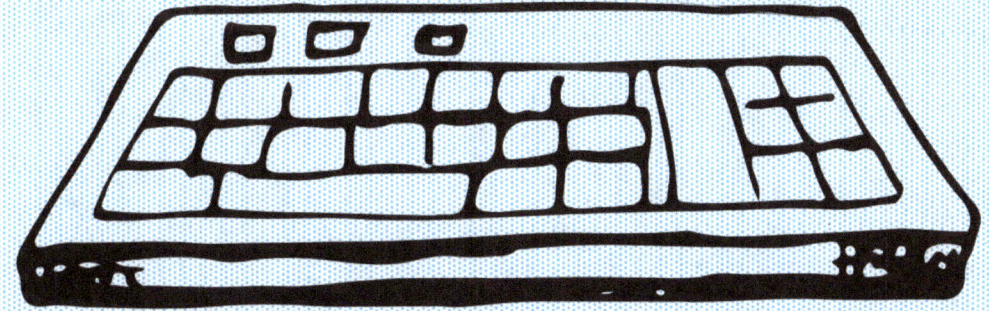

SNAPHAPPYMINDFULPHOTOGRAPHY.COM

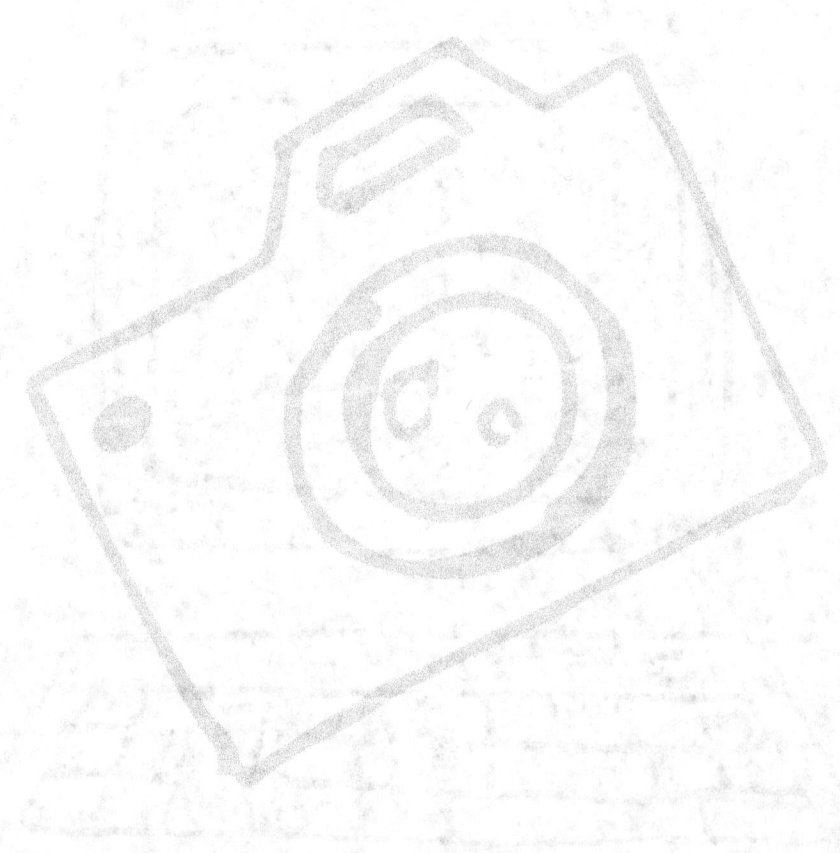

VISIT US ONLINE!

GALLERY!   **EDUCATOR IDEAS!**

MORE ACTIVITIES!   **ONLINE CLASSES!**

STORE!

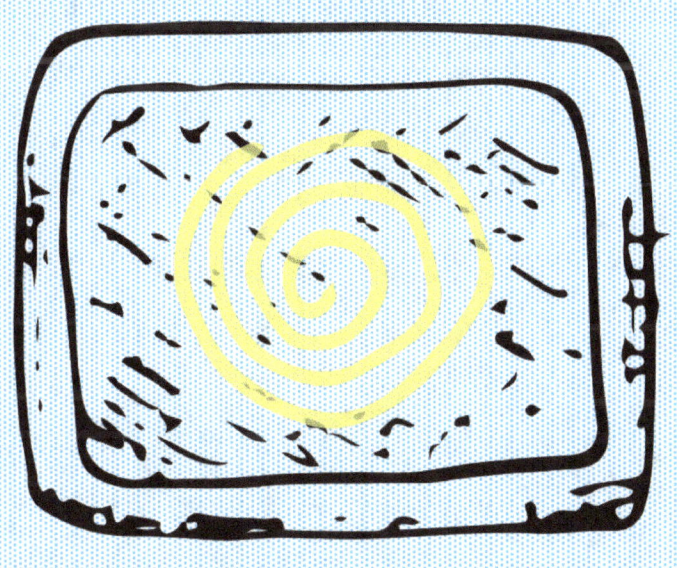

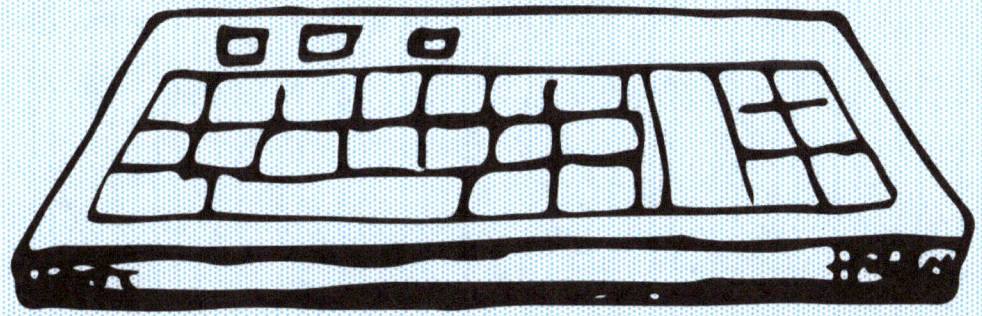

SNAPHAPPYMINDFULPHOTOGRAPHY.COM

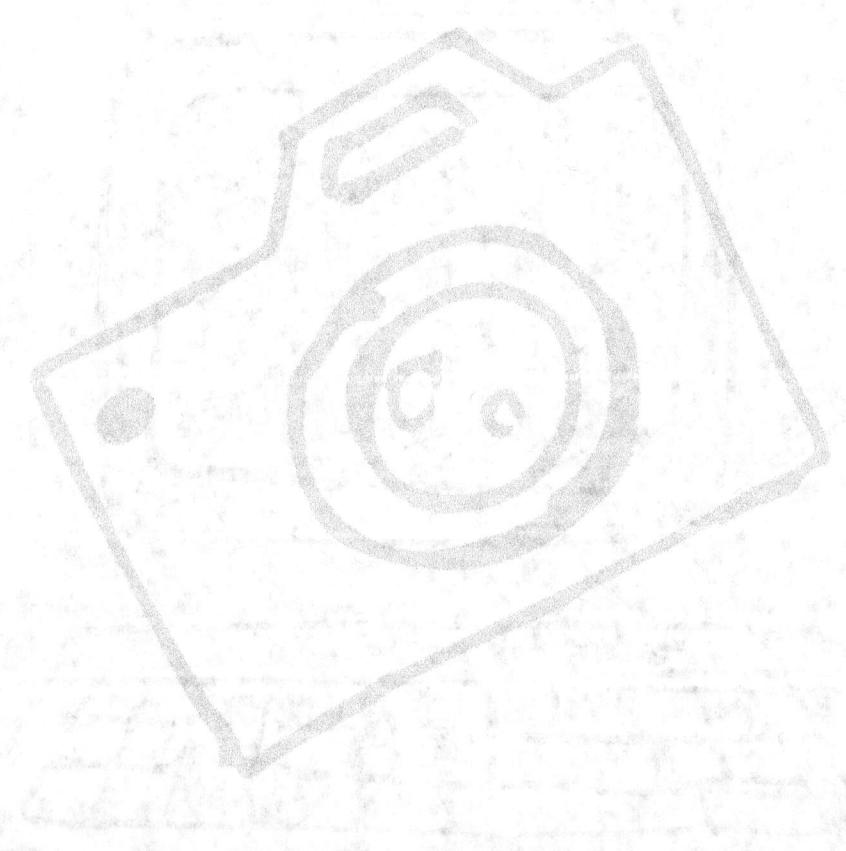

www.ingramcontent.com/pod-product-compliance
Lightning Source LLC
Chambersburg PA
CBHW062355220526
45472CB00008B/1810